D0669172

HOW TO BECOME A MULTICULTURAL CHURCH

How to Become a Multicultural Church

Douglas J. Brouwer

William B. Eerdmans Publishing Company
Grand Rapids, Michigan

Wm. B. Eerdmans Publishing Co.
2140 Oak Industrial Drive N.E., Grand Rapids, Michigan 49505
www.eerdmans.com

23 22 21 20 19 18 17   1 2 3 4 5 6 7

ISBN 978-0-8028-7393-4

Library of Congress Cataloging-in-Publication Data

Names: Brouwer, Douglas J., author.
Title: How to become a multicultural church / Douglas J. Brouwer.
Description: Grand Rapids : Eerdmans Publishing Co., 2017.
Identifiers: LCCN 2017008128 | ISBN 9780802873934 (pbk. : alk. paper)
Subjects: LCSH: Church. | Church and minorities. | Cultural fusion. |
    Church attendance. | Communities—Religious aspects—Christianity.
Classification: LCC BV600.3 .B75 2017 | DDC 250.8—dc23
    LC record available at https://lccn.loc.gov/2017008128

Contents

Foreword, by Wesley Granberg-Michaelson   vii

Introduction   1

1. Rediscover the Meaning of Home   15

2. Reconsider the Church's Name   31

3. Learn to Lead (Differently)   46

4. Be Theologically Generous   62

5. Seek to Understand— as Well as to Be Understood   80

6. Learn the Language   96

7. Move Beyond Cultural Stereotypes   112

8. Consider What the Flag Might Mean   127

9. It's Not the Music (or the Worship Style)   141

CONTENTS

10. It's the Meal (Where Strangers Become Friends) 157

Afterword, by Richard A. Davis 172

Acknowledgments 176

Foreword

Authors usually write books without knowing the context that will exist when they are published. Sometimes a book appears in print that seems remarkably timely and relevant, but the author could not have predicted that when writing it. It can almost seem providential, like a gift provided through circumstances beyond anyone's clever control.

That's the case with this book by Doug Brouwer. Neither he, nor anyone, could have predicted the political and social climate existing by the time *How to Become a Multicultural Church* would arrive in bookstores. But a shaking of the foundations of prevailing, assumed multicultural commitments in several Western democracies has convulsed political life. Most dramatic was the election of Donald Trump, whose campaign and executive actions targeted those who were "different," whether refugees or well-established immigrants, and manipulated legitimate economic anxieties of a dislocated white working class.

Demographic voting patterns revealed more dramatically than in any previous election the racial divide in the country. The "81 percent" became the frequent and stunning point of reference, indicating the percentage of white evangelicals supporting Trump. But among evangelicals of color, the percentage more than flipped. The same pattern held true, though with somewhat different percentages, for Catholics, mainline Protestants, and others. Forces in the election galvanized racial bigotry in stark ways rarely seen in recent times.

The trend is evident not only in the U.S., but also in European Western democracies, where Brouwer carries out his ministry. Hostility toward immigrants and rhetorical appeals to preserve "traditional" English culture fueled the stunning passage of Brexit. And the political climate in the Netherlands, Germany, France, Hungary, and elsewhere has been jolted by an unexpected revulsion toward immigrants and others changing what is perceived as the homogeneous cultures of such countries. These movements champion resurgent nationalisms defined by various versions of ethnic homogeneity.

In all this, multicultural life in modern, democratic societies is under an unexpected attack. Forces thought to be confined to the extremes, like guerrilla fighters in remote mountains, have been sweeping toward capitals of power, and in some cases taking control. Extremism threatens to become mainstream, reshaping how social contracts are understood, overturning conventional political discourse, and intensifying social and cultural tensions.

One may wonder what Brouwer's winsome, honest, and inspiring account of the International Protestant Church in Zürich, Switzerland, has to do with any of this. The answer is, a lot. In my view, the witness of the gospel in the world, and the focal point for God's mission, always has its roots in the local congregation. Lesslie Newbigin put it best when he said, *". . . the only answer, the only hermeneutic of the gospel, is a congregation of men and women who believe it and live by it."* If the witness and power of Christian faith is to be understood in the public square, it must be seen in the life of congregations shaped by its truth, just as it was first incarnated in a person.

That's why *How to Become a Multicultural Church* is not some "how to" manual for tinkering with congregational life. Rather, it's a survival guide for congregational witness in today's world. The book is rooted in the journey of a single congregation, uniquely positioned and comprised, striving to be a faithful "hermeneutic" of the gospel. That story is then amplified by Brouwer's diverse pastoral experience, and by his fresh biblical interpretation and practical examples, which sustain this journey and will inspire others.

Multicultural congregations in the U.S. are slowly growing. Defined by a now-familiar benchmark—at least 20 percent of participants in the congregation are from a racial group other than the dominant majority—they now comprise an estimated 13.7 percent of congregations. Yet, U.S. congregations are far behind the curve of changing demographics in society. For instance, the large majority of congregations are far less racially and culturally diverse than the schools their children attend, which is one reason why millennials often walk away from a church that doesn't come close to embodying the diversity they now assume and value in society.

Today, trying to become more multicultural is emerging as almost another congregational fad. Increasingly desperate for survival, congregations are likely to try anything. It's another in a list of pragmatic rejuvenation strategies, like increasing parking. What's missed is that becoming more multicultural is no strategy at all, but rather at the heart of the church's identity, and key to its missional potential.

Brouwer reminds us that building a worshiping community that crossed the boundaries of race and culture, first between Jew and Greek, became definitional of the New Testament church. That's how people understood the reconciling power of the gospel. Further, the church's mission to the world had its congregational roots not in Jerusalem, but in the church at Antioch, a dramatic example of a multicultural congregation. Such a living body of believers was, and is, a hermeneutic of the gospel.

We are now living in a time when true racial reconciliation and a shared multicultural life in society are questioned as not really being possible, and even undesirable. Such convictions, put plainly, are an affront to the gospel of Jesus Christ. They challenge directly the credibility and truth of Christian faith. So, the challenge is urgently raised, how is the church to respond? The answer must begin by a determination, simply, to be the church. If the messages of social evil which fuel racial and ethnic division in society are to be countered by the church, it must begin not simply with rhetoric, but with the demonstration that another social reality is possible.

The question, then, of "How to become a multicultural church" can be reframed as "How to give witness to the gospel in today's world." That's how to begin reading this book.

The congregation in Zürich, which provides a reference point for this narrative, is shaped, through geographical realities and spiritual mysteries, by the dynamics of world Christianity. In the world today, 244 million people have moved, or are moving, from one country to another for a wide variety of reasons. About half of this number are Christians, even though Christians comprise only one-third of the world's population. The unrecognized story of global migration today is the massive movement of Christians which this entails.

This can, and should, dramatically impact congregational life. In a city like Zürich, with an international population, Christians from all corners of the globe seeking a church home visit the International Protestant Church. It's a microcosm of a dramatic global story. As author and friend Jehu Hanciles says, "Every Christian migrant is a potential missionary."

Brouwer describes what it's like to pastor, nurture, and sustain such a multicultural congregation. He gives keen attention to crucial elements like leadership, stereotypes, organizational dynamics, worship style, language, theology, national loyalties, youth, and much more. All these become signposts in his navigating of this journey, born out of experience and illuminated with practical wisdom. His lessons, frustrations, and joys become a curriculum for others.

It should come as no surprise that *How to Become a Multicultural Church* finds a center in the practice of hospitality, and the sharing of that meal where the presence of Christ is the shared gift of grace. "Loving the stranger," the actual translation of the Greek word for hospitality, is nearly becoming the act of a counterculture in some Western democracies. The church must discover and nurture those practices which build such an alternative culture and provide a bedrock for our witness in the public square. The story in these pages, with its humility, honesty, and joy, provides a glimpse of what is possible. We should digest this wisdom, and then, in our own varied places, go and do likewise.

WESLEY GRANBERG-MICHAELSON

Introduction

I began writing this book when I was five years old.

The church in which I grew up, like a lot of churches at the time, supported missionaries all around the world. The worldwide missionary movement, which had begun in the previous century, was still going strong.

Occasionally these missionaries would pass through while they were "home on furlough" in the United States, and they would tell stories of their work. And I remember being taken not so much with their words, since they were rarely effective speakers, but rather with their slide shows and with the idea that someone I knew might actually live in a place like Nigeria or South Korea.

Someone in the congregation with a basement woodworking shop had the idea of making a large map for the church social hall, a map showing all the places where these missionaries lived and worked. This person even went to the trouble of electrifying the map. In other words, when you pressed a button—for Lagos, Nigeria, for example—a light became visible on the continent of Africa. One of our missionaries actually lived there!

I loved to play with that map. I suppose it was an early version of interactive learning, and it was remarkable for 1960, but it still required a great deal of imagination. What would it be like, I wondered, to serve a church, to tell people about Jesus, in Africa?

But I never made it to Africa.

I have traveled there, of course, several times, as I have traveled to lots of places around the world, but I have never lived and worked in Africa, which is sort of what I thought—it was all a little vague at the time—God would call me to do. Instead I became a pastor in the United States. And I followed God's call to exciting, if not terribly exotic, places like New Jersey, Illinois, Michigan, and even Florida. (Compared to other places I have lived, Florida is actually quite exotic, but that's another story.)

I grew up in a conservative Christian culture where movie going, card playing, and dancing were expressly forbidden. Those activities, we were told, might not be bad in themselves, but they frequently led to "other things," worse things. To tell the truth, I was never much of a dancer or card player, so I never chafed under those restrictions, but the prohibition against movie going was a problem. Movies for me definitely led to "other things." Movies opened my eyes to the world around me, and once I knew about that world, once I saw pictures and images from that world, I wanted to explore it, to get to know it.

The electronic map was for me a little like movie going. Once that map was hung, some little child like me was bound to imagine himself going to a place like Lagos . . . or Zürich. Parents should take more care before allowing electronic maps in the church social hall.

Eleven o'clock on Sunday morning

For the first 30 years of my ministry I served churches that were predominantly, overwhelmingly, even disturbingly white. ("Disturbing" because I was aware that the people inside the building seldom looked like the people in the surrounding communities and neighborhoods.) In other words, I served churches over the years with people who looked like those I had known all my life.

The advantage of a ministry like the one I have known, I suppose, is that I usually knew my people. In fact, I knew them very well. And of course they knew me. We had learned our Christian vocabulary together. We had memorized our customs and habits. We knew what to expect from church and from each other. We were rarely surprised.

Sameness, predictability, safety—these were important, cherished values to us. Not biblical values, certainly, but important values just the same.

Every year the churches I served in the U.S. would be required to fill out a questionnaire for the denomination about the membership. And every year, year after year, we would report that we were 99 percent white.

Why not 100 percent? Well, when the committee to complete the denominational questionnaire gathered to answer the questions, we thought we recalled having seen an Asian person once or twice. The spouse of a member maybe? Korean? Anyway, just to be safe, we told the denomination that we were 99 percent white. No church I have served over the years has looked exactly like the neighborhoods and communities in which the churches were located. Instead we always segregated ourselves along racial and ethnic lines.

Martin Luther King Jr. had many gifts, but surely one of them was forcing Americans to face some unpleasant facts about themselves. In 1968, just days before he was assassinated, King said to a congregation gathered at the National Cathedral in Washington, D.C.: "We must face the fact that at eleven o'clock on Sunday morning when we stand to sing 'In Christ There Is No East or West,' we stand in the most segregated hour of America."

His words stung, but apparently not enough for Christians to do much about them. Most of us weren't sure what to do. We knew that what he said was true, but—really—what could we do about them? And so, for a long time—longer than what was right or healthy—we did very little, except guiltily filling out our reports each year.

At a church leadership retreat a few years ago, our facilitator encouraged participants to dream about the future of our church, and one of the dreams our elders listed was "a more diverse church." And not only did we list it, but the idea attracted a surprising amount of energy. When we thought the best thoughts about ourselves, we imagined ourselves to be diverse, racially and ethnically.

But the facilitator pushed back. She said, "Really? Is that what you want? Do you have any idea what would be required to get there?"

The thing is, she never really said *what* would be required, but we apparently had active imaginations that day. Maybe she was right, we thought. Maybe diversity came with a high price tag. Maybe diversity would require changes that would be—how should I put it?—uncomfortable.

To fully appreciate how remarkable this discussion was, I should mention that we were considering a 16-million-dollar building campaign at the time. And somehow *that* didn't seem nearly as out of reach as a more racially and ethnically diverse church.

We quickly erased diversity from our list of congregational goals.

One recent study of churches in the U.S. defined multicultural churches as those where no racial or ethnic group amounted to more than 80 percent of the congregation. Using that rather imprecise but telling standard, *only eight percent* of all Christian congregations in the U.S. can call themselves multicultural.

Mainline congregations, the kind I have served over the years, came in below that average, and Roman Catholic churches came in above, with about 20 percent of Catholic parishes claiming multicultural congregations.

The times they are a-changing

But all of that seems to be changing. Whether we like it or not (and many people do not). Whether we are prepared for it or not (and many people are not). The racial and ethnic composition of our country —"our complexion," you might say—is changing. And our churches are changing as well.

Often these churches with racial and cultural diversity are new. In other words, they started out with the *intention* of being racially and culturally diverse. Others are older, more established churches that set out to look more like the neighborhoods and communities in which they find themselves. But the truth is, as I plan to explore in a subsequent chapter, not all of the change is intentional.

Some of it is happening whether or not congregations want it. No plan for change, no leadership retreat to set the goal; instead a slow evolution within the membership. Here and there a new nationality, a new ethnic group, a new language. What I experienced in my childhood—sameness, predictability, safety—still exists today in many, many congregations, but—and this is important—in a *decreasing* number of them.

One pastor, writing not long ago in *Christianity Today*, says this about his church: "Even though we weren't aiming for it, my first church was a multicultural church. It wasn't necessarily intentional—we just reached out to our poor neighborhood and that's who lived there."

Not all multicultural neighborhoods, however, are poor neighborhoods. Many neighborhoods—rich *and* poor—are becoming multicultural.

According to the U.S. Census Bureau, the U.S. is currently 17 percent Hispanic, 13 percent African American, 5 percent Asian, and almost 78 percent white. (For mathematicians, it is important to note, as the U.S. Census Bureau puts it, that "people may choose to report more than one race group.") According to the Pew Research Center, the U.S. is approaching a kind of multicultural tipping point within the next few years, so that whites will no longer constitute the majority. Dates vary for when this change will likely happen, but 2050 seems to researchers to be a conservative guess.

What "multicultural church" means

I should define my terms here, though the truth is there is no agreed-upon definition of the "multicultural church."

When people of various national backgrounds, racial/ethnic groups, and skin colors live and work and worship together, what you have is something that could be called "multiracial" or "multiethnic." The church I serve in Zürich, Switzerland, is certainly diverse racially and ethnically. Most Sundays, I look at my congregation and think, "This must be what God had in mind for the church on that first Pentecost— 'Parthians, Medes, Elamites, and residents of Mesopotamia, Judea and Cappadocia, Pontus and Asia, Phrygia and Pamphylia, Egypt and the parts of Libya belonging to Cyrene, and visitors from Rome, both Jews and proselytes . . .'" (Acts 2:9–10). It takes my breath away.

What I have in mind when I use the term "multicultural church," however, is something more—more than an unexpected mix of nationalities, races, and skin tones. A multicultural church will not simply have people who are African-American, but African-Americans who will engage to some degree their African-American cultural backgrounds, traditions, and norms. A multicultural church will not simply have people from South America, but South Americans who will identify with and intentionally engage with Latino culture. A multicultural church will not simply have second-generation Asian immigrants, but second-generation Asian immigrants who to some degree still engage and embody Asian cultural norms.

So, one key to this definition is that a multicultural church is more than a mix of nationalities and races and skin tones, but also a mix of cultures. But there is more. To be a multicultural church, in the sense I have in mind here, also means that these diverse cultures will not only live and work and worship side-by-side, but they will also try to do all of these things together, engaging with each other, making decisions together, trying their best to understand each other, and often irritating each other with their vastly different ways of looking at the world.

A multicultural church, therefore, is one where there is *an intentional engagement of cultures*, not just a mix of races and nationalities.

A country like the Netherlands, to take a helpful example, has recently been described as being tolerant rather than multicultural. The sheer variety of nationalities and races and skin tones on the streets of a city like Amsterdam, for example, is obvious to anyone who travels there. What is not so obvious is whether the various nationalities and races in that country are finding ways to recognize, accommodate, and support each other.

The criticism often leveled at that country—and several others in Europe—is that these cultural groups are hardly as integrated as they could be and perhaps need to be. They exist together, they inhabit the same land, they may even work together in the same offices and labs and classrooms, but they are hardly intentional about their life together. Leaders of countries like Germany, Great Britain, and France have gone on record as saying that their multicultural efforts have failed.

On the other hand, a few other countries around the world—Australia, New Zealand, and Canada come to mind—have claimed considerably more success with being multicultural. In these countries, so we're often told, each minority culture makes a substantial contribution to the larger culture.

I use this discussion merely to illustrate my specific interest here, not to debate public policy. It's a hugely controversial topic. There is, in Europe and elsewhere, a rising tide of nativism, a strong and sometimes troubling pushback against immigrant groups, a feeling that newer immigrant groups simply do not integrate well.

My interest is much more narrow.

The term "multicultural church," as I understand it and plan to use it here, implies something more than being tolerant or even welcoming, it implies more than living closely together or even demonstrating the ability to get along. It implies nothing less than attempting to be the church of Jesus Christ together and in the process finding ways to honor and embrace and even celebrate a variety of cultural backgrounds.

The multicultural experience of my life

I am no longer sure what I expected when, at the ripe old age of 59, I accepted the call to become pastor of the International Protestant Church of Zürich, Switzerland.

Sure, I expected to live and work abroad, something that I had always dreamed of doing, ever since I got my hands on that electronic map at church. But what I experienced from my first Sunday here was so different from anything I had ever known that I feel compelled to understand it, to write it down, to put it into words. I knew from my first worship service that I had found something extraordinary—not perfect, mind you, but extraordinary—something that needed to be described for others who would find themselves making this same journey toward a multicultural church.

On my first Sunday here I had no responsibilities, and so I did something that I seldom have the opportunity to do. I sat in the congregation and worshiped along with everyone. I sang the hymns, I prayed the prayers, I listened to the sermon, and I went forward for communion—without any responsibility for anything other than my own worship.

And when it was over, when the pastor had given the benediction, when the organist was playing the postlude, for which we all sat and listened, my wife leaned over and whispered, "That was awesome!"

And it was. Truly, unexpectedly awesome. I had tears in my eyes. And not for the last time.

I have worshiped in churches all over the world—Haiti, the Dominican Republic, Israel, the Philippines, South Africa, and Peru. I have even preached in a few of them. And I can truthfully say that I have never in all my years of church-going experienced anything quite like this.

Waiting in line to receive the bread and wine of communion at the International Protestant Church of Zürich, I could see around me Africans, Asians, Indians, Europeans, and even a few, though not as many as I expected, North Americans like me.

I could see every skin tone God ever imagined.

Introduction

I didn't know what to wear that first Sunday, so I wore what I had always worn to church—a dark suit with tie, my uniform—but I learned that morning that the dress code for worship around the world is more varied (and colorful) than I ever imagined. There were one or two other dark suits and ties like mine, but some of the women from Africa and India wore colorful dresses. Or maybe they weren't dresses. But whatever they were, they were colorful.

As I made my way to coffee hour, I thought, "God, I am not prepared for this. I realize that I wanted it, and even prayed for it, but I know that I am not prepared for it. Why did you answer this particular prayer about serving a church like this—and not so many other heartfelt prayers I have offered over the years?"

Of course I know that every person God has ever called to ministry— and to most other vocations, for that matter—has had similar thoughts and questions. And I know from my theological training that one of the signs of an authentic call is the overwhelming feeling of inadequacy that comes with it. Think of Moses ("I am slow of speech and slow of tongue"). Think of Jeremiah ("I am only a boy"). I know all of that. But still.

Here I was, about ready to assume the role as pastor of an international church, and for the first time in many years, for the first time since my ordination 30 years ago, I had no idea how I was going to do what I had been called to do. What in the world was I going to say to these people?

As it turned out, I need not have worried. They had plenty to say to me. When I was tongue-tied, they were not. Almost as soon as that first worship service was over, I heard many voices asking for, often demanding, my attention. I wasn't always sure what I was being told, so I listened more carefully than I have listened in years.

And that careful, thoughtful listening, though I didn't fully appreciate this on the first day, would become an essential component of leadership in a multicultural church.

What follows

In the chapters that follow is the story of one person's journey into the multicultural church. It is my attempt to explain why multicultural churches thrive. Not all of them do, of course, but the one I serve does. Why is that? It thrived before my arrival, and unless I make a mess of things, it will thrive after I am gone.

So, it's not me. And it wasn't the pastors who came before me, though all of them did fine work, and I am grateful to all of them for preparing the way for me. In the same way I hope to do my best to prepare the way for those who come after me.

If it's not me, then what is it?

I have identified a number of factors—actually 10 of them, mostly because 10 is a nice round number —that I believe contribute to the life and vitality of a multicultural church. There could be more than 10 factors, but I have observed at least these 10. I have given these 10 careful thought. And I have explored these 10 with others who are familiar with the multicultural church.

My experience with the multicultural church is mostly limited to the International Protestant Church of Zürich. The setting, I realize, is Swiss, not American. Switzerland has a state church, the *Landeskirche*, and the U.S. most emphatically does not. (The church I serve is not part of the state church.) Having served churches on both sides of the Atlantic, I am very much aware of the vast differences between churches in Switzerland and the U.S.

But I believe that the situation here, the extraordinary experience of so many cultures coming together and somehow finding a way to be the church, could be instructive for churches in other places, especially in the U.S.

I should acknowledge that there are many churches around the world like the International Protestant Church of Zürich. In the 1950s and 1960s, mainline churches in the U.S. founded churches like the one I serve in a variety of cities around the world. Often—at least at the beginning—these were churches for American expatriates, people who worked for a period of time away from home and were hoping while they were away to worship with like-minded, English-speaking people. A quick Internet search reveals that these churches now exist throughout the world—not just in Europe, but in Asia, Africa, the Middle East, and South America as well.

Many of these churches are small with only a few dozen members. A few, though not many, have enjoyed dramatic growth, with several hundred members. I became aware just this week of an English-speaking international church in Dubai with more than two thousand members and more than a thousand people attending worship each week. Most of these churches have no church buildings of their own. Many, like the church I now serve, are content to rent space offered by other churches. And some—the American Church in Paris and the American Church in Berlin are two churches that come to mind because I have spent time in them and worshiped with their congregations—have beautiful church buildings of their own.

What all, or almost all, of these churches have in common, however, is an increasingly multicultural congregation. Often what began as a mostly American congregation has evolved into something more. Today there is only one U.S.-born elder on the church board—or council—of my church in Zürich. The rest are from Hong Kong, the Netherlands, Germany, the U.K., India, Kenya, and of course Switzerland.

I believe that these churches have a great deal to teach the American church about being the church in a multicultural, multiethnic, multiracial setting. If, as seems likely, the U.S. continues to become more and more racially and ethnically diverse, then it makes sense to take a careful look at what churches like my own have learned—both our successes and our failures.

My story is personal

And while this is an attempt to understand why multicultural churches thrive—and of course why some do not—it is also a personal story, a very personal and at times difficult journey, which as I mentioned began with the electronic map and all of the messages I received as a child about a world larger than the one I knew.

One way to undertake a project like this, of course, would be to do it analytically, with studies, research, charts, and graphs. I suppose there is a place for a study like that, and I hope someone will do it one day because God knows that it's needed.

What I have in mind, however, is something different, something far more personal. This is my own story. In the end, I hope this approach will be more helpful than an academic study would be. After all, working in a multicultural church will always be an intensely personal experience, something that can't be measured, charted, or graphed. Working in this context inspires joy and wonder, the kind I experienced on my first Sunday here, but it triggers irritation and anger as well. You name it, I have felt it, at one time or another.

Misunderstandings in a multicultural context abound, occasionally humorous, as we'll see, and occasionally not. Some experiences have hurt deeply.

Prior to my arrival, some members of the International Protestant Church of Zürich learned that for a few years I took yoga classes. In my personal blog, in fact, I jokingly described myself as "a yogi"—which was humorous, I thought, because a 6'3", 210-pound American man is not the image that comes to mind when most people think of a yoga practitioner assuming pretzel poses on a tiny mat. How clever of me.

While my American readers might have been amused by that mental image, some members of the church here, especially those born in India, were not. They demanded to know what the search committee was thinking when it selected me to be their candidate.

I have offended church members in the past, and I will most likely offend others in the future, but I had never offended any before actually meeting them, before even arriving in their city. This was a new experience for me, a harbinger of other experiences that were to come.

My explanation—on the day I was introduced to the congregation—that yoga in the U.S. is mainly a fitness craze, with yoga attire and accessories being a multi-billion-dollar industry, did little to undo the damage. I even explained that my favorite yoga teacher was a born-again Christian who attended an evangelical megachurch. That didn't seem to help much either.

As it turned out, the yoga controversy was only my first encounter with multicultural differences that have the potential to cause harm in a church. I quickly removed the language about being "a yogi" from my blog, and I tried my best to understand how a Christian born in a Hindu culture might view yoga.

But I have to mention that I was also angry, especially when it appeared that nothing reciprocal appeared to be happening. Was anyone trying to understand the experience of an American pastor, trying to avoid the usual problems (for American pastors) of obesity, hypertension, and diabetes?

So, what I learned, among other things, was that this new church experience would not be easy. I would be finding my way in a far more complicated church culture than I had ever experienced before. This new church was going to require every ounce of energy I had. And then some.

To tell this story *without* making it personal, *without* confessing the inevitable frustrations and irritations, would be to miss crucial elements of the story.

Rich American expatriates

One more thing.

When I first moved to Zürich and tried to describe my new church to friends back in the U.S., a few of them said, "Aren't your members all rich bankers?"

Well, it's true that Zürich is the banking capital of Switzerland, and it's also true that several members work in investment banking and financial services. A couple of them manage hedge funds. But the membership of my church is not only diverse culturally and racially, it is diverse socio-economically as well.

Some of my members are teachers—at state schools as well as at international schools which serve the expatriate community. Some of my members are students, either Ph.D. students or postdocs at one of two nearby universities. Some of my members are au pairs, living in Switzerland on a short-term visa, working for a family, trying to experience life in another culture.

Still others are barely surviving. Switzerland has a social safety net that must be among the best in the world, but even at that some of my members have a difficult time making ends meet each month. Our congregational care fund makes regular gifts to those who need help with food, rent, transportation, medical care, and more.

One of my members is a recently arrived political refugee from Ethiopia. He has worked for the last three years to bring his wife and three children to this country—and to safety. He was an accountant in Ethiopia, but his job in Switzerland is far below his skill level. He doesn't seem to mind, though I know he must. Once his family is back together, they will create a new life together in a new home. Their new government will not intimidate, imprison, or torture them.

In other words, not all rich people. And not all poor people. Most are somewhere in between.

On any given Sunday morning I look out at one of the most culturally diverse congregations in the world today. And we are thriving.

How come? That's the story I want to tell.

CHAPTER ONE

Rediscover the Meaning of Home

I always thought the "Where is home?" question was innocent enough, and until I served an international, multicultural congregation, I asked it often and without a second thought.

"Where are you from?" Hey, just being friendly!

If you ask me where my home is, I'll say, "Michigan." I think of Michigan as home. My mother lives there, as do my sisters and their husbands and some extended family. Beyond that, I vacation there just about every summer, and I even have plans to retire there.

So, yes, "Michigan is where I'm from," I say, holding up my right hand to indicate that my home state is shaped like a mitten with its own thumb. I might even point to the fleshy part of my palm and say, "Right there. That's where I'm from." (This can be a puzzling gesture for those who do not call Michigan home.)

The German language has a word for this relationship between a person and a place. It's *Heimat,* and like several other German words it doesn't have an exact counterpart in English. German-speaking Swiss, the people I live with, often say *Heimatort,* which essentially means the same thing. Though *Heimat* and *Heimatort* have mostly positive connotations, they are emotionally charged words and can elicit a range of responses. Swiss passports list *Heimat* rather than a place of birth, even if it has been a few generations since someone has lived there, because, well, *Heimat* tells you more about a person. If you ask a German-speaking person where *Heimat* or *Heimatort* is, you'll need to set aside time for the answer and have plenty of tissues nearby.

For a growing number of people around the world, and for a growing number of people in our churches, the honest answer to the "Where is home?" question would be, "It's complicated." It's like *Heimat*. Often it takes time.

The answer to the "Where is home?" question is so complicated, in fact, and occasionally so emotionally fraught, that I have very nearly stopped asking the question altogether. Never mind that one of the first sentences that beginning German students learn is, *"Woher bist du?"* (Or, more formally, *"Woher kommen Sie?"*)

Where are you from?

Michigan

If you know where I'm from, then you know just about all there is to know about me. I say that Michigan is my home not so much because I live there (I don't), but because Michigan reminds me of who I am. Michigan has become for me shorthand for describing all of my essential characteristics—Midwesterner, descendant of Dutch immigrants, reserved, shy, thrifty, modest, not given to much spontaneity, but rather sober, serious, and dependable.

And of course Christian.

I suppose you could say that Michigan, more than anything, is my spiritual home. Over the years I have come to think of it that way.

Maya Angelou, the late American poet, once wrote (in the fifth installment of her autobiographical series *All God's Children Need Traveling Shoes*) that "the ache for home lives in all of us, the safe place where we can go as we are and not be questioned." I like that, and I agree that the "ache for home" exists in all of us. I feel it myself most days. And I believe that it is, more than anything, a spiritual ache.

Recognizing this powerful longing for home, the Roman Catholic Church in the U.S. developed a "come home for Christmas" marketing campaign a few years ago that I thought was especially moving. I felt a sudden rush of tears each time I saw the ad. At its heart the campaign was an invitation—or maybe a plea—to those who had drifted away from the church to return, to come home, to be reunited once again with their core identity.

I have no idea how successful that campaign was, but at the time I thought it was exactly the right idea. I'm not even Catholic, but that year I felt as though I wanted to go home, to join the great company of exiles who would be returning home for Christmas.

Coming home promises something more than coming to the place where there is a roof over our head. Coming home, as Maya Angelou points out, means coming to a "safe place." What that means, as she expresses it, is a place we can go and "not be questioned."

Maybe it's just me, and my own spiritual ache, but I hear in those words a no-matter-what quality, a kind of unconditional acceptance. Home is where you can have any crackpot idea you want to have—and not be questioned about it. Or more realistically, where you can be loved in spite of your crackpot idea.

Home is where you find love in spite of a lot of things. But home, as it turns out, has a few other connotations as well.

It's complicated

The teenagers in my church's youth group look and sound as though they have come from all over the world—India, China, Africa, even the Caribbean. But if you ask them where they're from—a question with which they seem to have a love-hate, though mostly hate, relationship—most of them will say that they're from Switzerland.

They were born in Switzerland, after all, and they have Swiss passports. Most of them attend Swiss schools. And among themselves, often to the consternation of their parents and sometimes their youth group leaders, they prefer to speak Swiss German. So, they may look as though they have come from many different places, but their home is Switzerland, every bit as much as home for me is Michigan.

It's the follow-up question that sometimes triggers a complicated reaction. If you say, "No, really, where are you from?" you are likely to receive a puzzled and possibly a pained look.

Pico Iyer, a British-born essayist and novelist of Indian descent, likes to say (as he did in a 2013 TED Talk about where home is) that, when people ask him where he's from, they "are always expecting me to say India, and they're absolutely right insofar as 100 percent of my blood and ancestry does come from India. Except that I've never lived a day of my life there. I can't even speak one word of its more than 22,000 dialects." Iyer left England as soon as he completed his undergraduate education, and after a few years in Japan has now lived much of his life in the U.S.

Where is he from? He would say, truthfully, that he's from the U.S., but everything about him suggests that the answer is just a tiny bit more complicated than that.

I am tempted to acknowledge that of course Pico Iyer is an extreme example, but my experience tells me that he's not. In my work, not just here in Switzerland, but in the U.S. too, I meet people like him often. His experience is actually becoming far more common than we might think, not only here, but also in the U.S.

And the "Where is home?" or "Where are you from?" question needs to be carefully considered, not least of all in our churches.

In 2015 there were 244 million people—or 3.3 percent of the world's population—living outside their country of origin (United Nations Population Fund, http://www.unfpa.org/migration), and the number is increasing rapidly. This number does not include those who have been internally displaced—in other words, many people are refugees within their own country. The majority of the 244 million cross borders (legally) in search of better economic and social opportunities. Others are forced to flee wars and persecution. About half of them are women of, as the report puts it, "reproductive age."

And some of these people, perhaps more than we realize, are even finding their way into our churches. Or they *might* find their way into our churches, if they knew that they would find a welcome there, a home.

A roof over my head

As it turns out, there are many ways to ask (and answer) the "Where are you from?" question. A more polite form of the question, depending on the context, might be, "Where were you born and educated?" A more direct question might be, "What passport do you hold?" And curiously, a few people at my church are always eager to ask, "Where do you pay taxes?" as though that might be the defining characteristic of home.

At a men's gathering soon after my arrival in Europe, and before I learned to be a bit more careful with the question, I asked the men to introduce themselves by telling me their names and where they were from.

When we came to one man, he said, "Home is wherever there is a roof over my head." I noticed that a few other men nodded in response, as though this was what men at their best should say. Practical and unsentimental. Home, according to this point of view, is wherever you happen to be at any particular moment.

But something about that answer troubled me at the time, as it does now, because it's much too glib. Frankly, it doesn't line up with what I have experienced in my own life, and more than that, it doesn't line up with what I believe. Home may well be the place where there is a roof over my head, but home has always suggested a great deal more to me than that.

Home, I think, refers to our identity—in other words, who we are at our deepest levels.

One time I asked a church member where home was, and suddenly her eyes filled with tears. She said, "In heaven." And at first I felt embarrassed for having asked the question, as I probably should have been, but then I realized that she was actually trying her best to give her pastor an honest answer, that she was grasping for an important truth.

Right now, she said, "I'm just passing through."

Which, I suppose, is true for all of us. At least some of us live with the vague feeling that we are in transit, not permanently settled, strangers in a strange land, ready to move on if we have to, or if the right offer were to come along.

A threatening question

One reason I no longer ask the "Where are you from?" question—or try my best not to—is that it can often sound hostile or even threatening.

I like the story that Barbara Brown Taylor, the American preacher, tells. She was walking one time near her home in the backwoods of rural north Georgia, when a man who was clearly not happy to see her, planted himself in her path and asked, "And who would your people be?"

She writes that she understood the question to be shorthand for "Why don't you get back in your foreign car and go back to wherever you came from?"

I wonder if the questions we sometimes ask of newcomers don't also sound threatening. Not as threatening as the person in this story, maybe, but threatening nonetheless, even when we think we're just being friendly and curious.

Too often, not always, "Where are you from?" sounds like "You don't belong here." And if people are looking for home, a spiritual home, then the last question they want to hear from their church is, "And who would your people be?"

An article appeared in a recent *Atlantic* (July 2014) with the title "Is It Racist to Ask People Where They're From?" The title, of course, was deliberately provocative. The article makes the case that in certain contexts the "Where are you from?" question can be more than threatening. Perhaps without intending it, we can—simply by asking the question—point out another person's "otherness."

What we might intend as an innocent question, as the article puts it, often has a way of hitting the ear at an odd angle.

A woman named Lorena from San Diego is quoted in the article as saying, "I'm multiracial and live in a very ethnically diverse city, but I was still asked this ["Where are you from?"] question SO. MANY. TIMES. while growing up. I never realized how ignorant and rude of a question it was until I became an adult. I can only hope no one asks my son this question. Because, really, the answer is simple: here."

Teresa from West Des Moines, Iowa, is quoted in that same article: "I am a Korean adoptee, raised in central Nebraska. I do not have an accent. I had a Swedish last name growing up and now have a Czech last name. I often get asked, 'Where are you from?' I say, 'Nebraska.' Then I get, 'Really, where are you from?' I have never self-identified as Korean-American and find it puzzling that people need to know this information. I do not know my biological family. I have a Korean adopted brother and growing up, we were often asked if we were REAL brother and sister (we are not biologically related). Is 'real' and 'biological' the same? Isn't family more than just blood relations?"

The day and the hour

I have always wanted church to be home. I have always wanted the church to be home for me. I wanted it to be more than that, of course, but I wanted it to be *at least* that. I have always thought the church at its best should be the place where we felt wanted and accepted, in spite of our shortcomings and deficits, in spite of how different we are from each other.

In the first church I served—I had not even graduated from seminary at the time—I had an overwhelming experience of unconditional love and acceptance—in other words, for me, of the church as home.

It was so overwhelming, in fact, that when people ask me "the day and the hour" when I was "saved," I usually point to that experience, even though there was never really a time in my life when I did not know that I was a child of God.

The people in that church loved each other in spite of everything and—this may sound odd—in spite of the ugliness and meanness and cruelty which seem to be present in every church, including that one.

And astonishingly—I wanted this, but never expected it—they loved me too.

I had no idea at the time that such a thing was possible, that such love within a church could be real. I had certainly never experienced it in the church of my childhood—or any other church, for that matter. Not to be critical of the church of my childhood, which after all introduced me to the electronic map, but by the time I reached adulthood I figured that it wasn't possible, that no church could demonstrate love like that.

And though the congregation I served during my seminary years could hardly be called "multicultural"—in the sense I am using the word here—it was certainly diverse, as diverse as any church I had known until that time. Sitting side by side in the pews were world-class surgeons and farmers, first-rate scholars and Amway distributors. It was a Big Ten university town, so there was bound to be at least a little diversity in that church, and there was.

Learning to speak meaningfully into this diversity wasn't actually as difficult as I imagined it to be at the time, but I still felt awed by the challenge of it. No, that doesn't begin to describe my feelings at the time. I was as scared as I have ever been.

The first time I preached in that church I visibly trembled on my way to the pulpit, clutching my sermon manuscript in sweaty hands. And then I preached what should have been an average-length sermon in something like seven minutes. I went so fast that several people glanced at their watches when I abruptly finished.

Even though I had been well-trained and had completed the required seminary coursework, I felt terribly inadequate when I found myself in an actual church situation. I couldn't imagine that I had anything to say that they might be interested to hear.

So, when I realized that they loved me and accepted me (in spite of the rather limited promise I demonstrated for ministry), I was overwhelmed.

I remember preaching a sermon one other time in that same church and having to stop in the middle of it because I was so overcome by the feeling of it, this thing I had not known before, this thing that every person wants and needs, but often doesn't know how to find. Tears are not a regular feature of my preaching, but suddenly there they were.

I didn't have the word for it then, but I learned later, with the help of a mentor and friend, to think of it as "grace." It was, I thought, maybe the most beautiful word I had ever heard. I fell in love with it. I even changed my vocational direction because of that one word and how it felt in my life. I wanted to be around it all the time, if I could only find a way.

Being a pastor was the last thing I wanted to be before this experience (what I thought I was attending seminary for is no longer clear to me), but after this experience, well, I couldn't imagine being anything but a pastor. I wanted other people to know what I knew to be true.

So, I know the day and the hour when I was saved, when I saw my life differently, but also the day and the hour when I came to think of the church differently, when I had a new (for me) sense of what the church could be.

Since that experience I have always wanted church to be home—for me, of course, but also for every person who might pass through its doors. Not just a home away from home, not just a roof over our heads on Sundays, but home in this more profound sense, a place of acceptance and unconditional love and grace, a place where aching hearts find safety.

Church as home

The churches I have served over the years haven't always felt like the one I found as a seminary student. Each one has had its own unique strengths and gifts. Each one has had its own wonderful, dedicated people.

But the quality of home, I now know, is a rare and precious thing. It doesn't come along more than once or twice in a person's life or ministry. I have seminary classmates who are nearing retirement age, and it seems clear to me from our communication over the years that they have never experienced anything close to what I have experienced.

I serve a church now—here in Switzerland—like the one I served all those years ago when I was a seminary student, a church that feels unmistakably like home, even though it's far from Michigan, and far from anything I would describe as familiar.

I can see that for many people in the church that it is a place of grace and safety. Lots of crackpot ideas, I have to say, are tolerated here.

The church I serve is far from perfect. That's not a criticism, just an observation, and I think most members would agree with me about it. All of the ugliness, meanness, and cruelty that you find in any church—and in any group of people—exist here as well. That may seem harsh, but anyone who has known the church as long as I have will know the truth of that statement. I wish it were not so, and I do my best to fight against it, but those things are here. And I'm afraid it will always be so.

Still, there is something here, something that was obvious to me from my first visit. This church is a place that can be called home, that feels like home, that has been home to a large number of people over the years. And I know that that's one reason, one important reason, why the church thrives, why the church can be home to so many different racial and ethnic groups, so many nationalities.

Last weekend a man took me aside during the monthly men's mountain hike to tell something that had been on his mind. I could see the tears well up in his eyes as he spoke.

He and his wife, he told me, had been members of the church for more than 20 years. (I looked it up later and found that the number was closer to 28.) He is from the U.S., and his wife is from Sweden, but at IPC they found a home.

Their children went to Sunday school, children's choir, and youth group at the church. He and his wife have each held all the leadership positions it is possible to hold. And even though he had received several job offers over the years, offers which would have required relocation, he turned them down because the church was vitally important in all of their lives. It was *that* important.

One distinct advantage

The church I now serve has one distinct advantage over all of the U.S. churches I have known. And I need to be clear about this too because this is critically important: **Most of the members of the church I now serve are looking for a multicultural church experience.** They came—and they stayed—precisely because of the international feeling they found at the church.

In other words, they came not for the experience of speaking and singing English in worship, or even listening to sermons in English, which I had guessed would be one of the key unifying characteristics of the church, but they came for the experience of cultural diversity.

They have found home not in a church of racial, ethnic, or cultural sameness, or homogeneity, but in just the opposite, in a church of sometimes staggering diversity.

Let me try to describe how this works.

The International Protestant Church of Zürich also has many members who are Swiss but who have married someone from a different national background. Switzerland has a tiny population (a little more than eight million people live here), but the Swiss are world travelers. And it is not unusual for the Swiss to bring home husbands or wives from another part of the world.

IPC began, at least in part, as many international churches do, as a church for expatriates, people who move to a new country, usually for a short-term business assignment, and then leave again. Slowly, though, over the last 50 years, this congregation has begun to serve a different population. Not expats so much as internationals, people whose home would be difficult to name, people who—to some, maybe—don't seem to belong here, but who nevertheless live here.

I have come to see that the thriving multicultural church begins with this desire, not for sameness, but for diversity. (People who have experience with a variety of racial and cultural backgrounds seem to have a difficult time going back to a situation with less diversity.) Not many of the churches I know in the U.S., even those that have come to embrace the idea of cultural diversity, have started with such a strong desire to be a multicultural church.

If you asked the members of my church why they belong to IPC, many if not most of them would shrug their shoulders and say, "Isn't this the way church is supposed to be?"

What's astonishing to me—even if it's not to everyone else—is that IPC members would give biblical reasons for their membership and participation. This, they would say, is the church described in Revelation 7: ". . . and there was a great multitude that no one could count, from every nation, from all tribes and peoples and languages, standing before the throne and before the Lamb."

Honesty compels me to add one further bit of information. As much as the members of IPC crave the diversity they enjoy, many of them still seek out what is familiar to them. Some of the church members from India, for example, gather regularly for worship in one or another's home where they sing hymns in Tamil and enjoy the food of their home country.

I am also aware that some of our African members from time to time attend an African church in Zürich where they find a worship style that is livelier than ours. Similarly, a few Chinese members will occasionally worship at the Chinese church, and I found out recently that there is also a Japanese congregation in Zürich.

When I first learned about all of this, I was not surprised. I suppose that if I found someone in the membership from Michigan, we would get together from time to time for no other reason than to talk about our home state and the sandy beaches and the beautiful sunsets. Someone who has been there will know what it's like to be there.

If you asked these church members—from India, Africa, China, and Japan—why they feel the need to do this, they would stumble in their answers, as they have with me. Though no one has spoken these exact words to me, the occasional worship among people who look and sound like them is about staying connected with what is familiar, with what feels like home. It is about the comfort and satisfaction that comes from the familiar, this longing that lies at the core of our being.

I mention all of this in part because it is fascinating to me and in part because it stands in contrast to the church in the U.S. and the longings and motivations that shape U.S. Christians. Many churches in the U.S. woke up one day and found that the surrounding neighborhoods had changed. The neighborhoods were once one color, one socio-economic category, one racial-ethnic group, and then one day they weren't.

And so, the motivation for these churches to change—and God bless them for undertaking the work it requires to do this—was to adapt to their new ministry setting. They started down the long path to becoming a multicultural church because faithfulness required that of them.

Or perhaps they did it out of desperation. Either way, they did it. And perhaps the motivation matters less than the result. We seem to sense what God is calling us to. We seem to know that the church at its best is catholic, with many tribes and nations and tongues.

And yet, the familiar has a strong claim on us, doesn't it?

We're doing enough, most churchgoers say

Sadly—I don't know another way to characterize this—most Christians in the United States today say that they have mixed feelings about their church becoming more culturally diverse. Some have been pushed into the effort because of circumstances beyond their control, such as a changing neighborhood, but few chose this path deliberately.

My personal experience of serving churches in the U.S. tells me that there is some interest in being more diverse, some realization that the status quo isn't quite right, that maybe the gospel calls us to something different, but according to a study conducted by LifeWay Research ("Sunday morning in America still segregated—and that's okay with worshipers," January 2015), more than two-thirds of those surveyed agreed with the statement: *"Our church is doing enough to be ethnically diverse."*

As if to emphasize the point, more than half disagreed with the statement: *"My church needs to become more ethnically diverse."*

And then here is where the research becomes more revealing—or more troubling. Those who identify as evangelicals are most likely to say that their church is diverse enough (71 percent), while whites are the least likely to say that their church should become more diverse (37 percent). African Americans and Hispanic Americans were somewhat more likely to say their church needs to be more diverse (47 percent).

I don't know how exactly to interpret these findings, and the researchers themselves offered few explanations, so the temptation is strong to speculate, to provide reasons why the results show what they do.

The church members I have known and worked with over the years in the U.S. have not been smug and self-satisfied. Yes, they loved their communities and took pride in their neighborhoods. They wanted me to love those communities as much as they did (and typically I did). But they were rarely uncritical. Most could readily see when the church no longer looked much like the neighborhood around it.

I served a church for more than a decade in suburban Chicago, and a survey taken early in my time there revealed that church members loved their community, were head-over-heels in love, in fact. Still, when I pointed out that the church was old and gray, while the neighborhood around the church was teeming with young families, so many that the local schools were bursting at the seams, church members were quick to agree that something needed to change.

Their response wasn't quite the response to Peter's sermon on Pentecost—"Brothers, what should we do?"—but they were at least open to ideas and suggestions about how to make changes. Eventually—and not without a lot of hard work—we began at last to look like our community.

One more thing

When the apostle Paul, in Galatians 3:28, writes that "there is no longer Jew or Greek, there is no longer slave or free, there is no longer male or female," I suspect that he was not advocating for cultural sameness, homogeneity, or even blandness in the church. He had something more interesting in mind.

More than likely, he was acknowledging the staggering diversity that existed in first-century churches and encouraging those churches he founded to remember that, in Christ, they were one people.

Over the years I've noticed that on Pentecost the story from Acts 2 is often linked to the story from Genesis 11 about the tower of Babel. And I confess that I have never understood the link. I preached on one story or the other, but never attempted to discover the connection.

I always assumed that the creators of the Revised Common Lectionary had something in mind, but whatever it was it was lost on me. Until recently.

In the Genesis story, those who spoke one language—the story tells us that at the time "the whole earth had one language and the same words"—were separated or dispersed when their languages were "confused." Suddenly, they found themselves speaking different languages, and as a result they were "scattered abroad from there over the face of all the earth." This was God's way of dealing with their hubris, their desire to "make a name" for themselves.

But on Pentecost something happened. Actually, a great deal happened, but among other things God began the work of bringing people together again—and not by introducing a single language for all to speak, but by giving the Spirit.

God gathered a people. God brought people home. And the miracle of Pentecost was that those people found unity in their diversity.

They still spoke a variety of languages, and they still looked and sounded different from each other. They still had a variety of skin tones. They still had their own customs and habits and foods and traditions. But they were drawn together—in the Spirit of God.

Their unity was in Christ. And that is where we are headed too.

Home.

CHAPTER TWO

Reconsider the Church's Name

For the first time in more than 30 years of ministry, I'm serving a church with the word "international" in its name.

It's the first time I've served a church with the word "Protestant" in its name too, but then I've always served "Presbyterian" churches and "Presbyterian" has always implied "Protestant" to me. So, what's most striking to me about the name of the church I now serve is that word "international." The International Protestant Church of Zürich.

It has an impressive look and sound, doesn't it?

Most of the churches I have served over the years have had the word "first" in their names, in addition to the word "Presbyterian." That shouldn't be surprising, since *most* Protestant churches in the U.S. have a "first" in their name. I read somewhere that "First Baptist" is the most common church name in the U.S., with over 5,000 churches known as "First Baptist."

"First Presbyterian" cannot be far behind.

The first church I served after graduating from seminary was the Pine Street Presbyterian Church in Harrisburg, Pennsylvania. (Naming a church after a location turns out to be the second most frequent way to name a Protestant church, according to studies on the subject.) Pine

Street was a large, downtown church directly across the street from the state capitol—or, as we rather cheekily put it in our newspaper advertising, "The capitol building is across the street from us."

Our crosstown rival—the other large Presbyterian church in the city—was Market Square Presbyterian Church. These two churches traded members over the years depending on the strength of their preachers, and each had fine music programs befitting large, downtown churches. We rarely did much together, except for our joint Maundy Thursday and Good Friday services. And I never thought much about church names in those early years of my ministry. I don't think many people did.

When people heard our name (or saw our newspaper advertisement), they knew pretty much all they wanted to know about us.

In Wheaton, after my church began to experience considerable growth (and after we decided to expand the footprint on our property), I found myself, along with the leadership, re-thinking everything about the church, including our name. I recognized for the first time that our name was more than a description. It was actually a kind of claim. In naming ourselves, we were announcing something about ourselves to the community.

So, what was it exactly that we were announcing about ourselves? That we were the first group of Presbyterians to get organized in Wheaton? As it turns out, yes.

Interestingly, the next Presbyterian church to be founded in Wheaton did not cooperate in the numbering plan. Instead of calling themselves the Second Presbyterian Church, they became the Hope Presbyterian Church. The nerve.

In nearby Chicago, however, churches regularly gave themselves a number. Fourth Presbyterian Church, now the largest Presbyterian church in the city, was simply the fourth to be founded there. I think the numbering plan in the city continued all the way to the Seventh Presbyterian Church, where the plan seems to have come to an end. It was a good run. There's a well-known Tenth Presbyterian Church in Philadelphia, but no eleventh as far as I know.

Let me go on record as being pleased that the idea of numbering churches seems to have run its course.

"First Presbyterian Church" was a fine name, I suppose, but during my years in Wheaton I came to see that it wasn't much of an announcement about our identity as a church. I noticed, for example, that newer, nondenominational churches around us were calling themselves "community" churches, with the Willow Creek Community Church in South Barrington, Illinois, being the largest and most prominent. "Community" sounds to me a bit more inclusive and welcoming, though there is still something indistinct and vague about it. What in the world do they teach at a "community church"?

Even so, I was jealous because those nondenominational, community churches seemed to carry so much less baggage. Fewer and fewer people seemed to know what "Presbyterian" meant, and those who did know weren't always enamored with everything we stood for. In other words, I was starting to see the limitations and perhaps even the obstacles in our name.

I remember meeting around this time with the Presbytery Executive, whose position was the closest Presbyterians will ever get to that of bishop, and I remember telling him how much I chafed at all the rules associated with being a Presbyterian. I thought my church could be so much more, if only we weren't weighed down by the heavy burden of the denomination, including the denominational name.

And his response, which I have not forgotten, was a question: "Doug, when have we ever said no to you?"

I heard that as a kind of challenge. In other words, "Go for it. Who's stopping you?"

In the end we didn't go for it. And we probably missed our window of opportunity. The church today is still known as the First Presbyterian Church, with all that that name announces and suggests and implies.

The limits of a name

But here's the thing: the name "First Presbyterian Church" never announced or suggested or even implied "multicultural." People who drove the heavily traveled street alongside our church buildings (and who saw our tasteful "First Presbyterian Church" sign) would have assumed that we were a typical, suburban, homogeneous congregation in the western suburbs of Chicago.

And they would have been right in their assumption.

I am troubled by that now, but I wasn't then. We were adding members, week by week, so what if they were all or mostly white? No one was complaining about our growth—except, of course, for the neighbors, who didn't like all the cars in their neighborhood on Sunday mornings.

Nearly everyone who came to us during those years was someone who looked a great deal like us. Incomes, educational levels, racial backgrounds, political opinions—we were astonishingly similar. And to be honest about it, we preferred it that way. What would have been our motive to change?

Our biggest (and loudest) disagreements were about music. And also whether or not to administer ashes on Ash Wednesday, a practice which was deemed "too Catholic" by some of our older members. Part of our identity, remember, was that we were Protestant, not Catholic.

When I complained about the lack of diversity early in my time at the church, my complaint was about the lack of *age* diversity. We were an older church. And our community was young. I identified that as our biggest problem, and—to the church's credit—we went about addressing it.

What I didn't see—and I am ashamed about this now—was that a lack of age diversity was only one of our problems. We lacked diversity in other ways too.

The temptation, of course, was to think that the community was mostly white. Everyone we knew was white, after all. In the neighborhood where I lived at the time, there were no black families that I remember.

Not a single one. So, we thought, we just happened to live in one of those areas where white people were in a decided majority. Not surprising, then, that our church would be all or mostly white.

Except that wasn't really the case. There was another racial group in the city, one we somehow missed.

John O'Melia

One of the members of First Presbyterian Church when I served as pastor was John O'Melia. He served on the search committee that brought me to Wheaton, and that's how I came to know him. I have written a great deal about him in a previous book, so here I will note simply that he opened my eyes, among other things, to the racial diversity in Wheaton to which I had previously been blind.

John was a nineteen-year-old soldier in the U.S. Army when it made its final push across Europe to defeat Nazi Germany. He told me several stories about his experiences in the war, but the one I remember best was the story about the day U.S. troops liberated the Nazi death camp in Dachau.

After helping to secure the camp, John remembers that he went off by himself to reflect about the horrors he had just witnessed. In his pocket was the New Testament that his mother had tucked into his belongings before he left for basic training and then for Europe. So, he grabbed the New Testament and went off to spend some time in prayer. His prayer, he says, was for God to use his life "to make sure that nothing like this ever happened again."

Of course, sadly, "things like that" continued to happen, but God nevertheless made use of John's life in extraordinary ways. After the war, John went to work for the YMCA, and in his role as director of the Cleveland YMCA, he organized the first-ever interracial summer camp, with black and white children attending together. In the 1950s, as you might imagine, this was a huge step—and not without controversy. But John pushed

35

ahead and became something of a legend in YMCA history. In time he was elected to the organization's hall of fame.

By the time I met John, his YMCA days were long behind him, but not his commitment to racial harmony and justice. I accepted his invitation early in my years in Wheaton to attend with him a Martin Luther King Jr. memorial service at the Second Baptist Church, an all-black congregation in Wheaton. I had been only vaguely aware of the church's existence until John told me about it. He and I were the only two white faces I saw in the congregation on that first visit, a Monday evening in January.

Over the next year, with John's gentle but insistent prodding, I came to know the pastor of the Baptist church, and through that friendship I was invited to participate in the service the following year. I continued to participate, and the service continued to grow (with a few more white faces each year), until during my last year in Wheaton the First Presbyterian Church hosted what had become by then the community-wide Martin Luther King Jr. memorial service.

At long last, if only for an evening, my church had become racially diverse.

Choosing a name

When the IPC was founded more than 50 years ago, I'm sure careful thought was given to the name they chose, but I wonder if the leadership at the time was fully aware of the implications of what they decided.

International churches once consisted primarily of expats from the U.S., employees of large corporations who with their families were spending a year or two in Europe and other parts of the world.

U.S. denominations like the Presbyterians and Lutherans helped in founding these churches, thinking of them as extensions of their work in the U.S. Some of these new churches, rather naturally, adopted names like the American Church in London or the American Church in Berlin.

Only later—when U.S. corporations began sending fewer employees overseas, for example—did anyone think to question these church names. The American Church in Paris, which traces its history all the way back to 1814, has a long-established reputation in the city and an extraordinary location along the Quai d'Orsay, so a change in name seems unlikely, and perhaps unnecessary, even though the congregation over the years has become decidedly less American and far more international.

The American Church in London, a much younger congregation by comparison, recently changed its name to the American International Church in London—to recognize, apparently, its U.S. origins while also acknowledging its changing circumstances.

IPC seems to have lost its American identity early on. The longtime members with whom I have spoken spent time in the U.S., but were not U.S. citizens. In other words, they were seeking, from the beginning, to be something more than an American church. They recognized the importance of the English language, of course, which is the language used locally both in business and in universities, but they also recognized that the church should include more than U.S. citizens.

As it turns out, it was an extraordinarily far-sighted decision.

Today, "International Protestant Church" comes up whenever a newcomer to the area does an Internet search for an English-speaking church in Zürich. Though there are a few other churches that come up with this search, IPC receives many, if not most, of these visitors and guests.

Worship in a language that most understand is important, but so is the message that comes along with it that there might be a place for me (and you).

That word "Protestant"

As thrilled as I am with that decision made long ago to use the word "international" in the church name, the second word in our church's name has taken me some time to understand. In the U.S. I'm reasonably certain that this word would not be one I would recommend (or feel comfortable with), but here I am grudgingly coming to see its importance and value. Culturally and historically, it makes sense.

Soon after my arrival in the country, I registered at the Gemeindehaus in Meilen—that's the city hall in the village where I live. I registered myself, my dog, and a few weeks later my car. When I leave, I will have to return to the Gemeindehaus and let the polite officials there know that I'm leaving and taking the dog with me. (The car will probably stay.)

The Swiss, as it turns out, like to know where everyone is at all times—nationals, but especially *Auslanders* (or foreigners) like me.

One of the questions I was asked that day at the Gemeindehaus was this: "Catholic or Protestant?" Without thinking much, I proudly said, "Protestant," half expecting and fully prepared to die for my faith. I was somewhat disappointed when I was not handcuffed and thrown into prison for this public profession of faith.

However, a few weeks later the tax bill arrived, and I finally understood the reason for the question.

Around two percent of my income, I learned, would be going to support the Swiss Reformed Church in the Canton of Zürich (Switzerland has 26 cantons or semi-autonomous states). If I had said "Catholic" that day at the Gemeindehaus, I would not have gone to prison either. Instead, a similar amount would have been deducted from my income and would have gone to support the Catholic Church in the Canton of Zürich.

And since the Canton of Zürich is overwhelmingly Protestant—I suppose I should thank the Swiss reformer Ulrich Zwingli for this—the Protestant churches around here are impeccably maintained and the clergy are very well compensated (or so they like to tell me).

Now, before my Swiss friends rise up to correct me on this point, I should point out that this tax is entirely voluntary. On that day at the Gemeindehaus I could have said, "Neither." And if I had, I would have had to pay no taxes at all (to the church).

So, why do the Swiss support their churches so well when so few of them attend on a weekly basis? That's a good question, and I don't know the answer. But I do have a guess: Swiss religiosity is actually deeper and more substantial than the typical American Christian might imagine. In a referendum a few years ago, the Swiss voted to keep the church tax. Given the choice, they opted to keep the state church at the center of village life.

For now, at least, I understand why it's important to keep the word "Protestant" in our name. We are identifying with a particular (and storied) faith tradition within our community.

Even so, an important part of our identity is also that we are not Catholic.

Risky business

Naming a church, as it turns out, is a risky business. I wonder, for example, how many Christ Community Churches out there really are . . . well, "Christ communities." With such a striking name, there must be some pressure to live up to it. At least I hope there is.

And renaming older, existing churches is probably even riskier. Journals for clergy frequently contain articles about "how we did it," and the renaming stories suggest that claiming a new or different identity can be a difficult and painful process. No wonder most churches stay with the old and familiar.

I recently came across research about the use of a denominational name showing that people have distinctly mixed feelings about denominational references, which I could have guessed. What I didn't fully appreciate was how mixed those feelings are.

When people see a denominational reference like "Baptist" in a church name, they are more than four times more likely to perceive that church as "formal" than if it had no such reference. Moreover, denominational references are three times more likely to make people see a particular church as "old-fashioned," "rigid," or "structured" than if there is no denominational reference at all. Finally, the lack of a denominational reference is three times more likely to lead people to feel that a particular church is "open-minded."

So, that would be enough for most of us to drop "Presbyterian" or "Baptist" or whatever from our church name, right?

Not so fast. Including a denominational reference in a church name, according to the same study, is more than twice as likely to help people feel the church is "honest." Conversely, excluding a denominational reference is more than twice as likely to give people feelings of uncertainty, and almost five times more likely to lead to thoughts that the church may be "trying to hide" what they believe.

I'm not sure what to say about this. I have never thrown my support behind the renaming of a church, even though I have thought, more than once, that a name change would be a good idea.

American pastor Gordon MacDonald, in a 2006 essay for *Leadership Journal*, has pointed out in connection with the renaming of his own church that name changes are relatively common in Scripture.

He notes, for example, that Jesus renamed Simon by calling him Peter, presumably to mold Peter into the leader he was expected to become. The early church gave Joseph of Cyprus the name Barnabas because Barnabas was a source of encouragement to all who worked with him. And then, perhaps the best known name change in church history, Saul of Tarsus became Paul. The chief persecutor of the church was to become the church's chief missionary.

It's no surprise that, when churches change something fundamental about their identity and mission, they would want to re-examine their names.

Welcoming the stranger

When the building project in Wheaton was nearing an end, the leadership recognized that something about our identity was changing. As our lead architect told us more than once, our new main entrance looked like "open arms" to the community. If we weren't going to change our name to reflect the change in our identity, what we were going to do to express this new way of thinking about our ministry and about ourselves?

In the weeks before the new building became available, I contacted the calligrapher Timothy Botts and asked him to design a mural for our entrance. I had been to a Catholic retreat center in Chicago and liked a small sign I saw at the reception desk: "When a stranger arrives, Christ is present."

And so, drawing on that experience, I gave our artist these words to use: "We welcome you as we would welcome Christ himself."

As I think back on this, I am appalled by how little thought went into the decision. I must have been young and inexperienced. There was no committee to think about it and no discussion at all that I recall. The building committee was more concerned with the color of the carpet than with the artwork I wanted to hang on the wall. They told me to do whatever I wanted. I passed around the proposed wording for the mural to staff members, and mostly I heard from them concerns about grammar and word choice, but not much else.

So, in the end, I just went ahead and did it.

I don't think I was even aware at the time that the little sign I saw in the retreat center grew out of the Rule of St. Benedict: "Any guest who happens to arrive at the monastery should be received just as we would receive Christ himself, because he promised that on the last day he will say: *I was a stranger and you welcomed me.* . . . Guests should always be treated with respectful reverence. Those attending them both on arrival and departure should show this by a bow of the head or even a full prostration on the ground which will leave no doubt that it is indeed Christ who is received and venerated in them. . . ."

As soon as the mural went up and was dedicated, I realized what I had done and panicked. What I had intended as a lovely sentiment was in reality a promise—and not just any promise, but a promise of *radical hospitality*.

And there it was—a massive mural, hanging in the entrance to our new church building.

41

When the Statue of Liberty went up in New York Harbor in 1886, I wonder how many people thought carefully about the words that were affixed to it: "Give me your tired, your poor, your huddled masses yearning to be free."

Was that a promise we as a country were prepared to keep? And for how long?

I seem to remember preaching a few sermons about hospitality in the weeks following the dedication of the new building. I was hoping that members would catch on. And mostly they did. Not because of anything I said, but because they tended to be an extraordinarily welcoming group of people. I think it was in their nature to be hospitable.

I don't suppose any of us knows at the start of something exactly what will be required of us. We put up a statue in a harbor or a mural in a church entrance, and we think more about the aesthetics of the thing than what the words really mean.

At wedding ceremonies, I ask couples to make promises to each other. "Repeat after me," I say: "I, ____, take you, ____, to be my lawfully wedded (husband/wife), to have and to hold, from this day forward, for better, for worse, for richer, for poorer, in sickness and in health, until death do us part."

And then we all say, "I do," as though those were the two easiest words in the entire English language. I certainly did not know what that particular promise would require of me. I suspect that very few couples do. We say the words, we smile, and then we hope for the best.

Christian faith asks us to give assent to all sorts of impossible promises:

"Take up your cross and follow me."

"Love your enemies and pray for those who persecute you."

"Whoever comes to me and does not hate father and mother, wife and children, brothers and sisters, yes, and even life itself, cannot be my disciple."

"Do not judge, and you will not be judged."

And now, this new one:

"We welcome you as we would welcome Christ himself."

At the beginning, it was easy and fun. The new building made us feel as though anything was possible.

But then the questions began to occur to me: What if people began to show up who were different from us? What if people of different backgrounds and colors and nationalities and sexual orientations began to worship with us? What if their ideas about worship and ministry and mission were not exactly the ideas we were comfortable with?

Would we welcome them as we would welcome Christ, or would we ignore them until they gave up and left?

Finding the holy in the unfamiliar

What Benedict surely knew when he wrote his Rule was that the members of his community needed to learn to find God in unexpected places—not always or even most often in the familiar places, but rather in the stranger, in the other, in the one who showed up unannounced and decided to stay.

I once heard a sermon about the two disciples on the road to Emmaus that forever changed the way I hear that story. The disciples of course thought that they were demonstrating hospitality by inviting the stranger to come in and join them for dinner. What they hadn't anticipated was that they would be changed by the stranger. The story tells us that in the breaking of the bread "their eyes were opened." The stranger vanished, but they were changed. Their lives would never be the same.

This is not the expected pattern. We like to think that by welcoming the stranger our good habits will rub off on them. We will be good for them. They will become more like us as they adopt our ways and habits and patterns.

We are almost always sincere in our welcome, and we want only the best for the strangers among us, but deep down we want them to blend in and fit the existing culture. We want them to thank us for our warm welcome. What we do not expect, and what we do not want, is to be changed in the process, to have our way of looking at the world be challenged.

Over the years I have been on dozens of mission trips. Most of them have been with the youth of the church, and most of them have been in the U.S. But a few have been with adults, and a few have been in places like Peru, Haiti, Israel, the Dominican Republic, and the Philippines.

I noticed from the first such international trip that Americans are proud of the way they do things. And not only are they proud, but they tend to think that their way of doing things is superior, sometimes vastly superior.

While building a house in the Dominican Republic on a hot August day, I found myself working alongside several Dominicans. Even though my home-building skills are woefully limited, I nevertheless thought my ideas were the correct ones in the moment. After all, my group was supplying the materials and most of the manpower, and so I expected the Dominicans would do things our way. They were extraordinarily hard workers, I thought, but I disagreed with some of their methods. I felt compelled to say so more than once.

It was only later, during the evening devotions and discussion, that I reflected on what had happened. Was it possible that there was something—anything—I could learn from them? That's seldom a question I think to ask. Maybe there is more than one way to build a house. Maybe the Dominicans could teach me a thing or two not only about house construction and hard work, but also about work and life itself. It is a lesson—I am not proud of this—that I have had to learn more than once in my mission work.

My way, as it turns out, is seldom the only way.

The word "church"

IPC is an international Protestant church, and proudly so. We like the way our name sounds. But our name does not always describe our life together.

Our habits and customs and ways of doing things are not always *inter-*

national. There is, most would agree, a decidedly American or Western bias in our attitudes and expectations (an important matter I will explore in the chapter about cultural sensitivity).

We like the title, though, and all of the good feelings that come with it, but we are often not ready to do the hard work required to live into our title. Who is?

Even calling ourselves "a church," I suppose, means that we aspire to something. But what? We are not a club, exactly. We are not a charitable enterprise, either. We are not even a group of like-minded people (we probably disagree about more than we agree about). So, what does it mean that we call ourselves a church?

I suppose it means that we are a people who are trying our best to follow Jesus—not only individually, but together. We do it imperfectly, which must be readily apparent to all who look in our direction, but we also do it passionately, fervently, sincerely, and most of the time as though our lives depended on it.

CHAPTER THREE

Learn to Lead (Differently)

For more than 30 years I chaired the church board at the U.S. churches where I served as pastor. At meetings of Session, which is what Presbyterians prefer to call their church board, I sat in the moderator's chair, and I led. Frankly, I like to be in charge.

I learned about leading church boards from one of the best. I was an associate pastor for the first five years after my ordination, and I watched as Fred Anderson, my senior pastor, led church board meetings with confidence and authority. I made lots of mental notes during those meetings, certain that my own day would come soon enough.

Fred and I often went out after the meetings too for what he called "debriefing," as though we had just completed a major military campaign. He certainly thought of board meetings in that way. By the time I became a senior pastor and moved into the moderator's chair, still in my early thirties, I knew how to lead the troops into battle.

Since then I have had many years to further develop and refine my leadership skills. This may sound like bragging, but the truth is these skills were once a requirement in the larger Presbyterian churches I have served throughout my ministry. Knowing how to lead a meeting in the Presbyterian church is very nearly as important as knowing how to preach a sermon or how to teach a Sunday school class.

Presbyterians pride themselves, after all, on doing things "decently and in order."

When I came to the International Protestant Church of Zürich, I came to an independent, nondenominational church with a congregational style of government and an often-unique way of organizing church life. What that meant for me, among other things, was that I no longer chaired meetings of the board.

I sit at the boardroom table, which consists of six tables pushed together in the church library, along with other board members. I have a voice in the business of the church, but for the first time since my ordination I do not have a vote. One of the elders is elected each year to chair the meetings. I am an advisory member of the board and I am expected to sit and listen.

From the beginning this has been for me a difficult and painful transition, perhaps the most difficult one in my move to this new church.

Since my arrival I have observed meetings that should have been concluded in an hour go to nearly three hours. I have listened as long discussions occurred around subjects like the annual church picnic. Should the church provide the meat for a barbecue or should the picnic be potluck? I sometimes went home not knowing—or caring—what had been decided. I have listened as elders launched into long, rambling verbal reports because they had not turned in the written reports before the agreed-upon deadline.

At times I felt like crying. Other times I tried not to roll my eyes. I often thought about what I would do—what I had been *trained* to do—in certain situations, but (mostly) I kept my mouth shut. I tried to remember that the congregation had called me, not because of my church board leadership skills, but because they wanted me to be their pastor.

As my employment contract puts it, "The Senior Pastor is in charge of the *spiritual welfare* [emphasis mine] of the congregation, including, but not limited to, conducting worship and preaching the gospel, pastoral counseling and visits, education of adults, youth and children, and the administration of the Sacraments (Ordinances) of Baptism and the Lord's Supper."

There is nothing in my contract about running meetings or leading the church board. The word "spiritual" in my contract seems to imply that the more worldly concerns of the church, like chairing board meetings, will be left to others.

I wonder how I missed that before I signed my name at the bottom.

Learning a new role

I must admit that seeing to "the spiritual welfare" of my congregation is not so bad. It is, after all, the work that I have always felt called to do with my life, that I remember signing up for all those years ago. Learning to lead a church board came later.

I can honestly say that this is the job description I have always wanted, but that doesn't stop me from thinking our board meetings are painfully slow and inefficient, even amateurish. I still chafe at the length of our meetings. I still find myself wanting to cut off discussion and move to a vote. And I still want to tell an elder who is making a long-winded presentation to make a motion, not a speech.

But something has changed in me. I have begun to see our work differently, and among other things I have learned that doing business briskly and efficiently, one of the values I learned early in ministry, is going to be far easier in a homogeneous, monocultural context. Getting work accomplished in a multicultural church is going to take time, sometimes lots of it. Meetings will almost inevitably feel unwieldy.

More listening, for example, is required as we try our best to understand each other.

I am not the only one who is frustrated with our meetings. I know because I have asked others on the board. No one with whom I have spoken wants to attend slow and inefficient meetings. But taking time

48

to understand each other now has a higher priority than speed and efficiency. This is work, I can see, that cannot be hurried.

Skye Jethani, in an article in *Leadership Journal* in 2011, has reflected on leadership in multicultural churches:

> Most of what I've heard or read about church leadership says we should fight tenaciously to maintain clear purpose, vision, and values within our organization. And recruiting other leaders who conform to these values. Allow too many people inside who hold divergent ideas and you'll derail the organization. But this mindset assumes that efficiency is the ultimate value to which all others must surrender. The best organizations, this view teaches, run like well-oiled machines with high capacity and high output. But in many cultures efficiency is not the highest good. And [some] leaders understand that in many cases clinical efficiency simply is not possible when seeking to lead diverse populations.

I think Jethani states the case well to people like me, leaders who have been trained in a particular style of leadership. As demographics shift and as churches come to terms with a new mix of racial and ethnic groups, a new mix of cultural norms and expectations, leadership styles will have to be re-examined, new ways of leading will have to be learned.

To listen to Jethani one more time: "If the dominant Anglo-American church doesn't start opening its ears, minds, conferences, books, magazines, and blogs to more global voices, it will quickly find itself unprepared for life in the post-American church world. But allowing diverse and divergent voices into the conversation is not only challenging, it's messy."

I could have saved myself from a great deal of anguish during my first year in Zürich if I had read those words at the beginning.

Benign paternalism

The truth is, there has been a great deal for me to unlearn, relearn, and re-examine, regarding the issue of leadership, including one matter that has long been troubling.

Several years ago, during a biennial meeting of the General Assembly of the Presbyterian Church (U.S.A.), I had the privilege of moderating a standing committee. Committees are important to the work of the Assembly because it is in committee, everyone seems to agree, where the "real work" of the Assembly takes place.

I remember being excited about the invitation. I thought it was an honor to have been asked. I experienced it as a confirmation of my leadership skills, and I was determined to do a good job. I applied all of my years of experience and training to the assignment.

The committee work went smoothly, we dealt with all of the business that had been assigned to us, none of it terribly controversial, and at the end of the week I made the report on behalf of the committee on the floor of the Assembly. Overall I remember feeling quite pleased and was ready to congratulate myself on a job well done, when one of my seminary classmates approached me.

As a member of the denominational staff, he had far more experience with General Assembly committee meetings than I had. He attended the meetings of my committee each day, in order to offer guidance to the committee and to keep track of certain items of business, and when our work was over, he decided to offer some unsolicited feedback on my leadership.

He was mostly complimentary about the committee's work, but I dismissed all of that as quickly as I dismiss a "thank you for your sermon" at the church door after worship. My friend then used a term to describe my leadership style that I would never have thought to use. He called my leadership style "benign paternalism"—a term I haven't forgotten.

He smiled as he said the words, and I did not hear them as a compliment. In the moment, I remember thinking, icily, "It's so good to meet up with you again after all these years."

I wasn't entirely sure at the time what "benign paternalism" meant, so I looked it up. There is no agreed-upon definition, but the term seems to refer to a male leader's use of power to control, protect, punish, and reward in return for obedience and loyalty. It means acting like a father to those who are not children in order to protect them from harm and to promote their well-being, as a father might define it.

As you might imagine, it's a widely tolerated leadership style, both in the church and in a variety of other settings, mostly because it seems to produce the right results, or because it gives the appearance of stability, not because those who are being led always like it very much.

Mostly I let my classmate's feedback nag at me. I suspected that it was true, though, and in the years since then I have become more self-conscious about my leadership—what I do and how I do it. After meetings, for example, I think about comments and directions and even gestures I made that could have been described as "benign paternalism." I always find something.

Interestingly—and this may in fact be a serious but unfortunate temptation for leaders trained as I was—"benign paternalism" may appear to be well-received, even expected, in a multicultural setting. For some people—typically not white Americans, who tend to prize their egalitarian culture—there is an expectation that the pastor will fill a certain role, will be perched on a pedestal, will act "fatherly."

Someone even said to me upon my arrival in Switzerland that what my new congregation really needed was a "strong father figure," someone who would bring order and stability to what was described to me as a bunch of unruly children. I nodded when I heard this advice, as though I understood what was being said, but the words hit my ear wrong, as they do now when I say them.

Certainly, the words "strong father figure" have a few positive connotations, and I shouldn't apologize for being either strong or fatherly. But there is something in the words that seems off to me, not in keeping with the earnest attempts I notice among the leaders of my church to listen to and understand each other, and not in keeping with what I believe about leadership.

It seems to me that when our church board is at its best, we are actively listening and seeking to understand. We are at our best when we find consensus among many competing ideas and viewpoints. We are at our best when we are able to break through cultural stereotypes and biases to get to the heart of an issue. We are at our best when someone says after a meeting that "the Spirit of God was present." I hear in those words the feeling that an authority outside ourselves was at work.

Don't get me wrong. I would very much like to be that fatherly authority figure, the one who is always wise, strong, and reliable. Over the years, in fact, I have tried my best to be that authority figure. But leadership in a multicultural context definitely requires something more nuanced, something hard to explain, something that unfortunately requires messy, inefficient meetings, but something that in the end feels right and is more in alignment with what I believe.

I am still navigating these treacherous waters, still trying to understand and grow, still learning when to be strong and fatherly and when to keep my mouth shut.

The leader in shorts and T-shirt

A couple of years ago, when the ALS "ice-bucket challenge" was in the news and going viral in social media—and everyone from politicians to business leaders to sports stars to entertainers was participating—I had the clever idea that I should accept my ice-bucket challenge after morning worship in full view of the congregation.

In the U.S. congregations I have served, this would have been a widely accepted decision. Someone would have said, I'm sure, that it was a great way to "humanize" myself in front of my congregation.

So, one Sunday after the benediction, I hurried out of the sanctuary, changed into shorts and a T-shirt, and grabbed a towel before heading outdoors. I had arranged for a member of the youth group to pour the ice-and-water combination over my head and someone else to make a video.

The congregation came outside more quickly than usual, like the shepherds in Luke's Gospel who hurried off to Bethlehem to "see this thing that has come to pass." And after I made a few comments about ALS and the importance of raising research money, the congregation was treated to the spectacle of seeing their pastor drenched with ice and freezing water.

Everything went as planned, and we even made a nice video of the occasion, but I should have known that, as with so many others things that first year, not every cultural group in the church would approve. Some people, I learned later, had mixed feelings about what happened. It's one thing if your favorite celebrity takes part; it's another if your pastor—the same person who just stood in the pulpit and preached the word of God—does it.

Some church members would prefer to have a leader who does not pour ice and freezing water over his head at the conclusion of worship. I see their point.

Culture of inclusion

I didn't see it when I first arrived, but my new church has done something remarkable, something that most other churches, as they make the long journey toward becoming multicultural, will undoubtedly have to learn. IPC has created within the church board what, in other contexts, is called a "culture of inclusion," a culture in which no racial/ethnic group, no nationality, no gender is privileged above another, in which cultural differences are recognized and taken seriously and not minimized. (In another chapter, I acknowledge that IPC has a clear dominant culture, which is western and American, but this culture of inclusion, I believe, is of a different order.)

When I first arrived at IPC, only one member of the board was from the U.S. The other board members were from Switzerland, the U.K., the Netherlands, Hong Kong, Kenya, and India. That diversity, I learned later, did not occur by accident. It occurred by design. The nominations committee is determined that the church board (we call it the "Church Council") be broadly representative of the entire church—not simply with a mix of older and younger elders, not simply with a good balance of male and female elders, but also, to the extent that it's possible, with elders from every racial/ethnic group and nationality.

The nominations committee, as you might imagine, has a daunting, if not impossible, assignment each year.

In other words, the church is determined that its multicultural character be visible from top to bottom. The diversity that is obvious on Sunday morning in worship is evident everywhere in church life, not accidentally, but purposefully and deliberately. The multicultural character of the church, you might say, has been imprinted on the church's DNA. It would be impossible at this point in the church's history to elect a church board made up entirely of North Americans or Europeans. The expectation for diversity in leadership has taken root. We don't know another way.

If I am honest, I must admit that there is still a fair amount of influence that the pastor has, even in this organizational structure. I am in the church office most days, after all, I lead staff meetings, I know the entire membership (not just narrow segments), and of course I have a microphone on Sundays and I like to use it.

My leadership of the church does not begin and end at board meetings. It never really did.

Every time I welcome the congregation on Sunday mornings at the beginning of worship, I set the tone and help to shape the church's identity. I tell everyone who we are and what we exist to do. I choose my words carefully, and over time I expect that those words will have an effect. Every time I preach a sermon, I announce the vision and direction that I believe God has in mind for the church. Every time I make a pastoral call, I represent not just myself, but the church, the whole body of Christ.

This authority is not incidental. But it is different from the authority I was trained to exercise. My understanding of authority, power, hierarchy, and influence has been challenged in this new situation—not diminished so much as redefined. And I can see that I am being changed, slowly and often grudgingly, but undeniably.

To be a leader in a situation like this requires a vastly different set of skills and sensitivities.

A peach among coconuts

One of the best ways I learned to navigate the cultural differences in my new congregation was through the peach and the coconut analogy.

The analogy is attributed to Kurt Lewin, a German-American psychologist who was interested in what he called the boundaries of public and private "life spaces." The outside layer of the fruit represents the person's public space and the inside the private space.

Switzerland and several other European and Asian cultures have what is called a coconut culture. In a coconut culture, people make a clear distinction between their neighbors, colleagues, and acquaintances on the outside, and their family and friends inside.

On the outside some people may not wish to give much personal information about themselves. They have a large private space on the inside because they share more about themselves there with people they know well. Their homes, of course, are part of their private space, and they are unlikely to invite people they hardly know into their homes.

Once people have moved past the outer layer, however, the commitment is long-term. I know that the Swiss friends I have made will be friends for life.

English-speaking cultures, on the other hand, are often peach cultures. Peaches typically share a great deal of information about themselves and behave in what seems like a relaxed, friendly manner towards a wide range of people. Peaches smile at strangers on the street and like to engage in small talk.

They treat new people (who are in fact strangers) as potential friends, talking to them openly and personally, as if they have already known them a long time. This lack of a clear distinction is also reflected in the preference for using first names with everyone, so that there is no obvious barrier to getting closer.

For peaches, homes are part of the public sphere, and so peaches are comfortable inviting people to their homes even when they hardly know them. The inner space of a peach is small in contrast to that of a coconut, and usually includes members of the immediate family, which is quite possibly the only group of people with whom they will maintain a close relationship for their entire lives. Other close relationships are not necessarily long-term. If you're a peach, you can be close for a while and then drift apart. That's the nature of a peach.

Americans are typically fuzzy and soft on the outside, and therefore are often perceived—in many parts of the world—as superficial and insubstantial. An American might say, for example, "Let's get together for coffee sometime!" We mean to be friendly when we say it, of course, but we don't always mean it literally. We sometimes fail to recognize that the other person, who hears the words differently, will go home and wait by the phone for an invitation.

The Swiss, as I mentioned, are more like coconuts—they have hard exteriors, but once you get to know them (the process may take several years), they become good and loyal friends. An invitation to coffee is an ironclad arrangement, not to be taken lightly. Only the exact time and location remain to be negotiated.

Even though I am from the American Midwest—and therefore somewhat reserved by nature—my style is still (surprisingly) perceived by other cultures, especially the Swiss, as more open, friendly, and gregarious than many are used to. At the beginning of my ministry here, my big smiles and hearty handshakes and attempts at small talk were often met with what felt to me like distrust.

Not all cultures are adept at (or find value in) small talk. Not all cultures smile broadly at total strangers. Not all cultures reach out and touch at a first meeting.

Relationships in a multicultural setting are exceedingly complex.

Some relationships take longer to develop. All of them require extraordinary sensitivity and alertness. Many cultures (not all) admire the American "can do" spirit, but this optimistic outlook on life—church life included—is not shared by all.

I now see that I cultivated a particular style of leadership over the course of my ministry, and it seemed to work well for me in a thoroughly peachy culture. I therefore had no motivation to question or change it. But now I live and work in a more or less coconut culture, where those earlier assumptions about what works and what doesn't continue to be challenged.

Third culture kids

I read somewhere that the most effective leaders in the future—in the church and elsewhere—will be so called "third culture kids," those who grew up or spent significant periods of their childhoods in other cultures. This was a term I had never encountered before my move, though in an international church I not only found myself hearing the term, but being surrounded by examples of it. IPC is filled with third culture kids (and third culture adults).

Third culture kids are the ones, it has been argued, who will be best prepared and attuned to the nuances of multicultural organizations, and that makes sense to me. After all, they have been navigating global and cultural issues all of their lives. Third culture kids sometimes grow up in a military family or as the children of missionaries. Some of the third culture kids I am getting to know at IPC are the children of business people and academics.

One reason third culture kids might turn out to be outstanding leaders in the future is that they have grown up with cultural diversity and see it as entirely normal. They accept change as part of life and have developed robust coping skills for managing change. Encountering a new cultural environment requires a highly specialized skill in order to understand that culture and adapt to it. Most third culture kids have been doing this their entire lives.

I can think of a few members of the youth group with one Swiss parent and one American parent, and the ability to understand both—to move back and forth between the language of each—is nothing less than astonishing. I see encouraging characteristics in these youth such as self-reliance, strong communication skills, adaptability, maturity, but I also see the challenges: being vulnerable to loneliness, a slowness to engage with others, and often the lack of a clear identity. Studies of third culture kids bear out these observations.

With his Kenyan father, American mother, and childhood years in Indonesia, U.S. President Barack Obama was in many ways a classic example of a third culture kid. Given his background and childhood, it should not be surprising that he would write a book like *Dreams from My Father* in which he comes to terms with his biracial origins. Arriving at a clear sense of his own cultural identity took years, and the circumstances of his childhood have been both a blessing and a challenge, as he readily acknowledges.

At the beginning of the year, when our pastor for youth holds an orientation meeting with parents, he sometimes provides a list of third culture kid characteristics. Each one begins, "You might be a third culture kid if . . ."

My favorite item on the list is "you might be a third culture kid if you speak three languages and can't spell in any one of them." A more poignant one is "You might be a third culture kid if you become anxious when the form you're filling out asks for a 'permanent address.'" Most parents nod knowingly as we move through the list. They are well aware that their children are growing up with both enormous advantages and significant challenges.

I see the third culture kids at my church as having the right backgrounds and experiences for leading multicultural organizations such as the church in the years to come. The adjustments they will make will not be nearly as difficult and painful as mine have been.

Moses and Jethro

Over the years I have led classes each year for new elders, deacons, and trustees, and the purpose of these classes was to get the newly elected leaders ready for their term of service to the church—in other words, to prepare them for leadership.

One biblical story I have often used—I always thought that it communicated the right message about shared leadership—is the story from Exodus where Moses receives advice from his father-in-law Jethro. As the story begins, Jethro sees that Moses is exhausting himself—"from morning until evening"—in the work of leadership (Exodus 18).

A wise father-in-law might want to keep most such observations to himself, but apparently Moses had a good relationship with Jethro, and so Jethro said, "What is this that you are doing for the people?"

I think the translation is that Jethro was not overly impressed with what he saw his son-in-law doing. Moses, to his credit, seems receptive to Jethro's observations and advice. Essentially, Moses shrugs his shoulders and asks, "What else am I supposed to do?"

Given this opening, Jethro doesn't hesitate. "What you are doing is not good," he says. "You will surely wear yourself out, both you and these people with you. For the task is too heavy for you; you cannot do it alone. Now listen to me. I will give you counsel, and God be with you!"

What Jethro proposes at this point is essentially a 1950s American corporate model with the people organized in a pyramid of "thousands, hundreds, fifties, and tens"—with only the most serious matters reaching Moses for a decision. To a Presbyterian from the U.S., this advice can only be heard as thrilling. Everything we in our mainline denomination hold sacred about leadership—a corporate, hierarchical structure—can be found in these verses!

As you might imagine, I was able to mine this story over the years for its humor, as well as its humble wisdom. I portrayed Jethro as a concerned father looking out for the interests of his daughter and grandchildren who were being neglected by a well-meaning but overwhelmed husband and father.

Looking back at this story years later, now from a multicultural perspective, I am surprised by how much I missed. Of course effective leaders delegate. Of course effective leaders are not micromanagers. Of course effective leaders organize teams. Of course effective leaders teach others how to be effective leaders. As Dwight L. Moody is supposed to have said, "It is better to set a hundred men to work than to do the work of a hundred men."

All of that still seems obvious and, frankly, not terribly profound.

What I seem to have missed over the years is something far more interesting and subtle—namely, the cross-cultural nature of the relationships described in this story. Moses had married a woman named Zipporah, who was not one of God's chosen people, and the man who gives Moses a lesson in leadership was a priest of Midian. I think this is a significant piece of the story, and I'm not sure why I never saw it before.

The people of Israel, generally speaking, did not establish many relationships with the other peoples of the region. In fact, they were warned repeatedly about keeping their distance, about not worshiping other gods. And yet here—in the narrow matter of leadership—the people seem to have found wisdom they very much needed to pay attention to.

As I think about it, the most difficult adjustment I have had to make in this new multicultural environment was not giving up my old role as chair of the meeting, though that was part of it. I think the larger difficulty was accepting leadership insights from a culture other than my own.

How do I put this? My experience in a monocultural, homogeneous church had led me to believe that there was one and only one way to lead, to manage. And letting go of that belief has been one of the most difficult challenges I have ever faced. I had to accept that there was something I could learn from a culture other than my own.

So, you could say that IPC has been my Jethro. I still think that my training and experience were good and useful. I am still grateful to Fred for the time he spent with me all those years ago. And I am not ashamed of my tendency toward being strong and fatherly. But what I have come to see is that in different cultural settings the assumptions supporting that training and experience will definitely need to be re-examined.

CHAPTER FOUR

Be Theologically Generous

If my account of the multicultural church has sounded mostly cheerful and enthusiastic until this point, then that tone is about to change.

Or at least it is about to become far more realistic and balanced.

Finding a way to be together—to do the hard work of ministry together—is extraordinarily difficult in any church, but I have come to see that it is even more difficult and very nearly impossible in a multicultural church. Perhaps this notion I have of the multicultural church somehow coming together is dreamy and romantic and impossible this side of glory. I don't know for sure. I would need a few more years here to form a better impression.

Right now all I know—I'll put this as bluntly as I can—is that the prospect appears bleak. The ties that hold a multicultural church together appear to be fragile. They shouldn't be—I'll come back to this— but they are.

Seeing people from so many national backgrounds gather for worship Sunday after Sunday is exhilarating. It never gets old. Serving them the bread of communion as they come forward one by one has been one of the high points of my life. I had goose bumps again yesterday.

But worship is just the starting point in church life. Worship is where we tend to look our best, and it's where we try our best as well. No wonder that our visitors and guests on Sunday morning are almost always amazed by what they find. Look closer, though, peek behind the scenes, and you will see the enormous difficulty of getting along, coming together, and finding areas of agreement.

Nearly all of my previous ministry experience was in churches where people not only looked alike, but came from similar socioeconomic and educational backgrounds. I suspect that if we had studied the matter, we would have found that voting patterns and political preferences were similar too. In other words, nearly all of my ministry experience—more than three decades of it—has been with people who viewed the world in pretty much the same way I did.

When I became pastor of a multicultural and international church, all of that similarity—and the assumptions that went with it—melted away in an instant. I am able to make very few assumptions about the people I lead. We have agreed to speak English, true, but even our common language turns out to be a surprisingly weak bond. Words that mean one thing in the U.S. can and often do have slightly different meanings or connotations in other settings.

A few weeks ago I led an adult Sunday school class in a study of C. S. Lewis's classic book *Mere Christianity*. After the second or third week, a class member from the Netherlands whose spoken English often puts my own to shame raised his hand and asked what the word "mere" meant in the book's title.

"It seems to suggest something less significant," he said, as though perhaps Christians shouldn't be reading this book. In that moment I became aware, in a way I had not been previously, that I could assume very little any time I taught a class or preached a sermon.

A small consolation is that in a classroom setting with 20–30 church members, it's fairly easy for someone to raise a hand and ask, "What do you mean by that?" In the act of preaching, no one (so far) has tried to do that, though there must be a word or phrase or strange American idiom in every sermon that leaves at least a few people puzzled.

Often, when I preach, I think I see puzzled looks on the faces in my congregation, as if to say, "What in the world is he talking about?" "What in heaven's name could he have meant by *that*?" I hope it's my imagination.

In fact, I try not to think too much about it when I preach because the effect would obviously be paralyzing. I now look at my sermon manuscript on Saturday—the day when I have always made my last tweaks and edits—and I try to hear the words I have written as members of my congregation will hear them. This a new exercise for me, a new stage in the editorial process, but it has become vitally important. I realize that I can no longer predict with much certainty what my church members will hear when I preach. I do my best to think about it on Saturday and not so much on Sunday.

Any preacher, of course, knows that this possibility exists in any preaching situation, not just in multicultural churches. Over the years people have heard—or claimed to have heard—all sorts of meanings in something I said that I never intended. What has changed for me is that the challenge has increased exponentially in a multicultural setting.

The ties that bind

For the first time in my life, I am no longer serving a church in a particular denomination or even a specific theological tradition. I grew up in the Christian Reformed Church in North America and graduated from the college of that denomination. I graduated from a Presbyterian seminary, and I was ordained in (and am still a member of) the Presbyterian Church (U.S.A.).

Most of my church members today could not say exactly what any of that means. My denominational background and membership is meaningless to them. It was mentioned at my introduction and seems to have been quickly forgotten.

After a wedding last Saturday, a member of the congregation who is from Poland approached me and wondered what a "Presbyterian" was. I mentioned during the ceremony that we were following the Presbyterian wedding rite, and I realized that I had unnecessarily raised a question in the mind of at least one person in attendance.

What I heard her ask was, "Who cares?"

To be accurate about this, denominational labels and ties were also becoming less and less important in the previous churches I served. In my experience people rarely joined one of my churches because of my church's denominational label. Early on I probably assumed they did, but I quickly learned the truth. People joined the church because we were "friendly," or they heard that we had "good children's and youth programs," or the building was prominently situated on a main street. That my previous churches were Presbyterian either mattered little to our visitors or was something we had to overcome. It was rarely if ever an advantage to be exploited.

Whatever denominational pride I had early in my ministry has been largely diminished over the years by the reality of church life in the U.S. Denominational labels simply don't matter as much anymore.

I remember teaching new member classes in previous churches I have served and thinking that the time I spent on what it means to be a Presbyterian was probably time that could better be spent on other matters. In those classes, people often, though not always, were brand new to the faith. They were curious about a great deal, which was exciting, but generally speaking they weren't quite as curious as I was about the difference between, say, Presbyterians and Methodists.

But if denominational loyalties don't hold us together, what does?

Early in my ministry at the International Protestant Church a church member told me something one of my predecessors was supposed to have said. "We believe," he said, "that Jesus Christ is our Lord and Savior, and we believe that the Bible is God's Word to us. Beyond that, we smile a lot." I know three of my predecessors, and it's difficult for me to imagine that any of them would have made this statement, except perhaps in a joking manner, and yet I realize there is some truth in it. We do mostly agree on the essentials, but it's the last part of the statement that presents our biggest challenge. What do we say about the rest?

"In essentials unity, in nonessentials liberty, in all things charity." This old saying always looks and sounds to me like a fine ideal, but the reality, I now know, is messy and problematic. Of all the challenges I have faced in serving a multicultural church, this would have to be the toughest.

Creeds and confessions

Having grown up in a tradition that valued creeds and confessional statements about the faith, I had always assumed that writing such a statement and then finding agreement with it were the ways that churches came together. We were Presbyterian because we agreed on the creeds and confessions of our tradition.

If anyone asked us what we believe, we could show them the statements that we agreed to.

I have occasionally tried to do just that. People would find our church's website and then look for a statement of faith, only to be disappointed. In previous years, I could proudly hand them a copy of the Presbyterian "Book of Confessions," containing the various creeds and confessional statements that the Presbyterian Church had decided to follow, dating all the way back to the Nicene Creed, and I could say, "That's where we stand."

I didn't really expect anyone to sit down and read the Second Helvetic Confession (to name one of the confessional statements in the book), but at least, I thought, the creeds and confessions would give a clue as to the theological heritage of my church.

Over the years, however, historical creeds and confessional statements, like denominational labels, seem to matter less and less. Fewer and fewer people seem to care—this is especially painful for me to admit—what the Heidelberg Catechism has to say. And so, many churches now publish their own faith statements on their web sites. Though these statements often have similar words and phrases, each one is clearly unique, having been written by a pastor or a church board to represent the views and stands of a particular church.

The church I now serve has no faith statement on its website, and there is no "Book of Confessions" that I can give away. Instead we have a "covenant" that pretty much acknowledges the staggering diversity within the congregation:

> Recognizing full liberty of individual interpretation, and taking cognizance of the various statements of faith under which its members may have made their professions, we, the members of this church, associate ourselves with all who follow Jesus, and promise to work with one another in this church to further its Christian testimony through worship and in service, supporting its efforts as best we are able.

As best we are able!

There are members of my church of course who believe we should go further than this, that we should declare ourselves, in particular, on the issues surrounding human sexuality. In their minds, we should strongly and unequivocally condemn homosexuality, as though the rest of the world is clamoring to know our stance on this matter. So far, though, no such statement has been written.

If pressed about our theological position, which we sometimes are, we would say that the church stands in the "Reformed" theological tradition. If pressed about that, we say that our pastors have, with only a few exceptions, come to us from the "Reformed" tradition. I realize, as we make these statements, that few if any people know what we mean. Because the church lies near the center of Zürich—and within a short walk of the church where the great sixteenth-century Reformer Ulrich Zwingli used to preach—claiming that we are "Reformed" makes some sense. The state church in Switzerland is called the "Swiss Reformed Church." And "Reformed" theology is what Zürich is known for. Also banking.

But these words and references no longer carry much meaning. Even my church members who live and work in the shadow of Zwingli's church would be hard-pressed to say what it means to be Reformed. And those who do seem to know what it means to be Reformed are often in disagreement. It is a heritage they do not claim for themselves.

Not long ago I preached a sermon about the David and Bathsheba story and mentioned, in what I thought was an off-handed way, that David's life could be considered a strong argument for the doctrine of total depravity. I should have known before I said it that no line during a sermon could ever really be "off-handed," because a person approached me after the service and asked to talk further about TULIP, the acronym for what are known as the "five points of Calvinism": Total depravity, Unconditional election, Limited atonement, Irresistible grace, and Perseverance of the saints.

He said, "I can probably live with 'total depravity,' but I have a hard time with the rest of it." Oy.

Infant baptism and believer's baptism

When the search committee interviewed me, prior to selecting me to be their candidate, they asked me, among other things, about my understanding of baptism. I gave a spirited defense of infant baptism, but said I could certainly get along with those who believed just as strongly in baptizing only those who were able to make a profession of faith.

I was naive in this answer, as I was in several others, but I thought I was on solid footing in a city like Zürich where Zwingli also defended the practice of infant baptism (and put several Anabaptists to death by drowning them in the Limmat River to demonstrate how strongly he disagreed with them).

As it turned out, the membership of IPC has representatives of several different positions on baptism. Those who believe strongly, as I do, in the baptism of infants are most likely in a minority, as a matter of fact, in spite of the church's claims to embrace the Reformed tradition. Or it may be that those who oppose the baptism of infants in favor of baptizing those "who know what they're doing" are simply more vocal.

Either way, the issue is far from settled.

In previous churches, I had the protection of my tradition. In other words, whenever the matter came up (and it did fairly often), I could say, "Well, this is the position of the Presbyterian Church." Today that protection, if I ever really had it, is now gone, and I find myself exposed. I am expected to give reasons for doing what I do. Hardly anyone, as I mentioned, cares about or understands my denominational affiliation.

A few months ago I made the decision to baptize the infant son of a couple who had not yet decided to get married. Their personal situation was complicated. But both of them—this was the critical issue for me—had agreed to raise the child in the Christian faith, whatever they eventually decided about being married to each other.

My decision to baptize the baby raised questions in the minds of church members who—I should have expected as much—were not at all reluctant to express them.

To me, though, the decision was relatively simple. My training and experience told me that baptism was about how this child belonged to God and not about the circumstances of his conception. I discussed the decision with several members of the church board—past and present. I felt confident that I was making the right decision. I went ahead.

In the end, it was my first direct experience with conflict in this church, and like most conflicts it was probably avoidable. I was aware in the days and weeks following the baptism that the topic was being widely discussed. I was getting calls both at the church office and at home. The associate pastor was getting them too, sometimes from the same people who were calling me. I heard the opposing opinions, and as often happens in these situations I did not hear much support for what I had done. The support was there, I felt, but it was not nearly as outspoken as the opposition. It never is.

On the bright side, this was (mostly) a theological issue.

Most of the people who have come to see me over the years have wanted to discuss far less consequential matters. "The organist plays the hymns too slowly!" "The custodian is not cleaning the kitchen!" "The children make too much noise when they leave after the children's sermon!" To be able to discuss a matter like this was actually—I can say this in hindsight—quite thrilling.

One couple made an appointment to see me "to discuss, you know, the baptism." We sat together in my office one Sunday after worship, and I expected the worst. I expected to hear them tell me how deeply disappointed they were in my leadership and pastoral judgment. If they were, however, they didn't say it. To my relief and surprise, we had an actual theological conversation. The couple had been well-trained. Their previous pastor—in Singapore, I think—had taught them well about the meaning and significance of believer's baptism (and of course about the utter nonsense of baptizing babies).

Given the circumstances of the parents' relationship, they asked, shouldn't I have advised them to wait until the child was old enough "to make the decision for himself"? What would have been wrong with simply "dedicating" the baby during worship and not calling it a baptism?

These were good questions. A baby dedication was not an option that I had considered, which I quickly acknowledged. I had never dedicated a baby. I told them that my training and background had led me to a different—and perhaps too hasty—decision to baptize the baby.

Here were two thoughtful church members pressing the issue in an articulate and respectful manner. Ordinarily I would have felt stressed and anxious in a situation like this, and instead I was . . . well, happy, strange as that may sound.

I am still mostly happy with how this conflict unfolded, though not entirely.

After doing my best to understand the position of those who strongly opposed infant baptism, especially in these unique circumstances, I did not find much evidence that anyone was trying to understand my own position. To make a church like ours work, to bring so many diverse backgrounds and opinions together, to expect to get along, requires that everyone do the difficult work of considering another person's point of view.

I was irritated, looking back, that no one else seemed to be doing what I was willing to do. If anything, theological positions seemed to harden. I felt a bit of bullying, as a matter of fact, as I often do when there is disagreement. Theological conversation is not our church's strength.

A generous orthodoxy

Thanks primarily to the American pastor Brian McLaren, the term "generous orthodoxy" has found its way into the vocabulary of American pastors and occasionally their church members as well. The term, as McLaren acknowledges, came originally from Hans Frei, a twentieth-century biblical scholar and theologian, and McLaren has appropriated the term as the title to his best-selling book.

I must say, there is something quite appealing about those words. On my best days I think of myself as both "generous" and "orthodox."

The subtitle to the book describes McLaren's project even more clearly: "Why I am a missional, evangelical, post/protestant, liberal/conservative, mystical/poetic, biblical, charismatic/contemplative, fundamentalist/Calvinist, Anabaptist/Anglican, Methodist, catholic, green, incarnational, depressed-yet-hopeful, emergent, unfinished Christian."

I suppose that these words could also describe the work of a multicultural church like mine. When we think the best thoughts about ourselves, we imagine that we are able to come together and celebrate the strengths of our various identities and backgrounds, different though they may be.

But, seriously, will it ever be possible to come together in this way? Can unity in Christ ever be affirmed in a meaningful way, while the distinctiveness of each cultural background (and viewpoint) is valued? Will our unity in Christ ever be more than a superficial unity?

I sometimes despair over these questions.

"We must never underestimate our power to be wrong when talking about God, when thinking about God, when imagining God," writes McLaren. "A generous orthodoxy, in contrast to the tense, narrow, or controlling orthodoxies of so much of Christian history, doesn't take itself too seriously. It is humble. It doesn't claim too much. It admits it walks with a limp."

In a multicultural church, I have noticed, not many people are willing to admit error. Not many are willing to admit that they walk with a limp. And far from taking themselves *less* seriously, my experience is that people in a multicultural church seem to double down on their convictions. It is almost as though those convictions are necessary in a setting where so many opinions and theories and beliefs are being expressed. As I mentioned in connection with the conflict surrounding the baptism, all of the generosity seemed to be my own. Convictions hardened, not softened.

My reading seems to confirm what I observe.

In her book *Leaving Church*, the American preacher Barbara Brown Taylor writes, "As a general rule, I would say that human beings never behave more badly toward one another than when they believe they are protecting God."

Robert Putnam, in his popular book *Bowling Alone,* and especially in his more recent writing, has concluded that "inhabitants of diverse communities tend to withdraw from collective life, to distrust their neighbours, regardless of the colour of their skin, to withdraw even from close friends, to expect the worst from their community and its leaders, to volunteer less, give less to charity and work on community projects less often, to register to vote less, to agitate for social reform more, but have less faith that they can actually make a difference, and to huddle unhappily in front of the television. . . . Diversity, at least in the short run, seems to bring out the turtle in all of us."

I can learn to love turtles. It's the bullies who are very nearly impossible for me to love. And even the best churches seem to have a few, the people who feel called to monitor and judge and correct the theological thinking of others, the people who in Barbara Brown Taylor's words believe they are "protecting God."

Fleming Rutledge, a well-known American preacher, has taken the term "generous orthodoxy" as the title of her website. There she notes that "we cannot do without orthodoxy, for everything else must be tested against it." I agree with that, but it is her definition of "generosity" that gets even more of my attention.

We must be generous, she writes, "as our God is generous: lavish in his creation, binding himself in an unconditional covenant, revealing himself in the calling of a people, self-sacrificing in the death of his Son, prodigal in the gifts of the Spirit, justifying the ungodly and indeed, offending the 'righteous' by the indiscriminate nature of his favor."

I have been deeply troubled and discouraged when members of my congregation do not seem especially generous, but most days I am not sure I can be generous in the way that Rutledge describes it. To be honest, there are probably few if any days when I am capable of that sort of generosity. God, certainly, but not me.

I grew up in a theological tradition that could not be "generous" with the Catholic church, that found itself a few centuries ago having to separate from the Catholic church. I come from a tradition that continues to separate whenever it finds views and beliefs that cannot be reconciled with its own version of orthodoxy. (As I write this, I count at least 30 different Presbyterian denominations in North America, a fact that cannot be considered a definition of theological generosity.)

So, my own cultural and theological background betrays me. My own background tells me that orthodoxy must always trump generosity. As happy as I am to be here in this multicultural congregation, as privileged as I feel to be able to do this work, as much as I want to engage in the theological conversation, I find the lack of a theological center to be my most difficult challenge:

- A week ago a church member sends me a link to a YouTube video of his favorite apologist, Ravi Zacharias, and asks me to take a look. "It will be the best 45 minutes of your day," he promises.
- Still another member confides that he became a Christian "overnight" by reading a book about young earth creationism by a German author, who is not a theologian but an engineer. "Please

read it so that we can talk about it together," he says. I reluctantly promise to do so.

• An elder sends me a link to what for him was an especially moving sermon by the American television preacher Joel Osteen. "Really?" I think incredulously, and then I promise to have a look.

• A visitor to the church, who is a Ph.D. student in a field of science I have never heard of, tells me how "powerful" Joyce Meyer has been for her as she has recently come to faith. "I know who she is," I say, noncommittally. And then I worry that my noncommittal answer may discourage this new believer.

• A young woman from China sat down next to me at a church member's birthday party and said, "The teachings of your church are unsound. I thought you should know how the community perceives your church." "Really?" I said. "In what way is our teaching unsound?" "Well," she said, "you once allowed a woman to preach." I wanted to mention that my older daughter is a very fine preacher, but resisted the temptation.

• A pastor from India whose goal is to plant 500 churches in the next few years will be coming to Zürich next summer, and a church member wants to know if I will let him "bring the message some Sunday" and tell about his work. "Let's take a look at the schedule," I say, wondering what I am committing myself to.

• A large women's Bible study group will be meeting in the fall to study the book of Revelation, and already they have exceeded their limit for registration and have started a waiting list. I do not recognize the name of the author of the study they will be using. "Why is this particular book of the Bible so intriguing," I wonder, "and not, say, Luke's Gospel?" I do not address this question to anyone in particular.

My head swims.

When I interviewed with the search committee, I carefully explained that I knew who I was and what I believed, thinking that this would be a strength in a multicultural setting. And in some ways it is. I could not have done this work earlier in my ministry, when my pastoral identity was still in formation. Today that identity is still forming, I suppose, but it is mostly set. I know who I am, and I know what I believe. I have what it takes to have the conversation.

But none of that is enough. My church is too ill-informed theologically to speak of a "generous orthodoxy." In my teaching and preaching I am finding that I must name what orthodoxy is so that we can be generous about it, so that we can have a meaningful conversation about it. I have a great deal of work to do.

A question of membership

IPC welcomes new members two to three times each year. These are typically classes of young adults, some of them with young children. These are happy moments in church life. And I especially enjoy them and what they mean about the health and vitality of the church. What happens on these occasions is that we ask the questions of membership, we pray, and then we hug and shake hands. The welcome lasts no more than a few minutes, but for me it is the high point of the service.

I came to IPC with an understanding that church membership is the beginning of something, not the culmination. In other words, in churches where I have served, people join the church to begin their Christian journey (and to join the rest of us in ours). There is no expectation, as there is in some traditions, that new members reach a certain level of knowledge or maturity in the faith before they are allowed to become members.

I once joked in a sermon that the church always sets the bar low for membership. I meant to be funny—and to my delight, there was laughter—but at some level the statement is true. The bar is low because people are responding to an invitation to become disciples. When they become members, they are not yet fully devoted followers. The hope is that that will happen in time.

When people become members of IPC, we ask that they believe in Jesus Christ as Lord and Savior. (In new member classes over the years I have carefully explained what those words "Lord" and "Savior" mean to us.) We also ask if new members "intend to be [Jesus'] disciple, to obey his word, and to show his love."

This—to me—is the language of starting out, with serious intentions, of course, but the questions have to do with embarking on a new way of life, a new identity.

So, it came as a surprise to me when an elder came to me before the last group of new members was welcomed to ask about the sexual orientation of one member of the group. Was he gay? "I don't know," I said truthfully. "If he is gay, would that disqualify him from membership?"

And that question set off the sort of conversation that churches all over the world seem to be having. If that new member had been known (or found out) to be gay, if we saw on his Facebook page that he was in a relationship with a man, would that information have disqualified him for membership? I thought the answer was obvious. It certainly was to me.

We talked for quite a while, and then we involved others in the conversation—mainly, members of the council. Everyone, it seemed, was uncomfortable with the conversation. It's tough, I remember thinking, to be orthodox and generous at the same time. I was discouraged.

In the end, the person who inquired about membership decided not to pursue the matter. I called, and he did not respond. I felt ashamed. I assumed that our long silence in getting back to him was all he needed to know about us. In any case, that was the end of the story. But not quite. The issue, I'm certain, will surface again. And I am already weary of the conversation.

Science and faith

I don't remember anymore what possessed me to say yes, but last fall I agreed to teach a class on science and faith, actually a series of classes. I spent the summer preparing and reading several books, more than I have for most such classes. But I was still anxious.

I was aware before I started that several church members saw science as a serious threat to their faith. Every new discovery seemed to chip away at the foundation of what they believe. These were the people, in fact, who had asked for the class. They wanted to know how they should respond to the challenges presented by science, how to speak to neighbors and co-workers who challenged and sometimes belittled them for their beliefs.

I enjoyed the preparation, since the topic was not one I had previously spent much time with, and by the time the class started I thought I was well prepared. One of the benefits of anxiety for me is the tendency to overprepare, and in this case I was glad I did. I spent the first fifteen minutes or so of the first class asking the class members to be respectful in their comments and observations. I told them that there was no single Christian point of view regarding science, and I promised to be fair in my presentation. My own position, I told class members, would become obvious, but I nevertheless wanted to make a balanced presentation—with young earth creationism, old earth creationism, intelligent design, theistic evolution, and even a movement called Biologos receiving thoughtful consideration.

The first class went well, but on Sunday afternoon I expected to find my email inbox overflowing with critical messages. None came. Instead, the response to the class was overwhelmingly positive. Because IPC is located near two major research universities, we have a large number of faculty, postdocs, and Ph.D. students in the membership. They seemed pleased, generally speaking, that the topic was being treated in a respectful manner. They also observed, accurately, that there was more faith than science in the presentation. (I told them that I try to stay with what I know.)

I can't begin to express how relieved I was by the response of class members. I felt as though I had found a formula for handling difficult issues in a diverse and multicultural congregation. Only one church member asked to see me so that she could tell me of her disappointment with the direction of the class. Even that, I thought, was mostly a good and helpful conversation.

The best strategy I have found for talking about theological beliefs in a multicultural setting is to be respectful about all beliefs—and those who hold them. As I told the members of the faith and science class on the first day, "Tell me when you think I am not treating your position with the respect it deserves."

The impression I have now, though, more than a year later, is that I will be less likely, not more, to tackle tough subjects in the future. The care that is required in a setting like mine presents a challenge, sure, but it also presents nights of worry. Should an adult Sunday school class about a difficult, but important, subject create such anxiety—not only in me, but in class members as well? And if a hard look at faith and science created so much anxiety, what would happen in a class about, say, the Bible and sexual orientation?

If we affirm Jesus Christ to be our Lord and Savior, and if we believe the Bible to be God's Word to us, then we should be able to talk about science and sexual orientation and just about anything else, shouldn't we?

Our differences, however, make these conversations very difficult. I find myself discouraged when I think about it. Some days I find myself thinking that it was a mistake to come here. It would be far easier to serve a church with like-minded people, the ones I have known all my life, the ones who look like me.

I remember an adult education course on marriage that I taught at a previous church. I was so excited about the response to this course, in fact, that I wrote a book about the topic. During that particular course, I left the topic of same-sex relationships to the end. And, not surprisingly, there was a fine turnout for that last class. I taught in the church sanctuary, and most seats that morning were filled.

The thing is, I did not feel anxious about teaching that class. Part of it—a large part, I suppose— was that I knew the class members. We were all part of the same theological tradition, we looked and sounded (and probably voted) alike, and so I knew their thinking on the subject and could anticipate their objections and the exact places where they would be uncomfortable. I slept well before and after the class.

I do not yet have that same sense of ease in this setting, but I have not given up hope.

Hope begins in the dark

The American writer Anne Lamott once wrote that "hope begins in the dark," a sentence I like to try to remember, especially when I struggle in my ministry to find the theological center.

This kind of hope is the "stubborn hope," she writes, "that if you just show up and try to do the right thing, the dawn will come. You wait and watch and work: you don't give up." And so, I find myself hopeful about the work of theological generosity, but it is most certainly a stubborn hope. I have to work hard not to give up. I have to work hard to look for dawn. I have to work hard to notice God at work among us.

Hope for me has always had its start in the early morning when I'm not quite sure what I'm seeing or what is happening, when there's a lot more doubt and confusion than faith. I imagine that this is what the world felt like on that first Easter morning. You don't really get to belief, you don't really know what's happening, until the sun is high overhead. So, the best you can do, until things are sorted out, is to "wait and watch and work."

I hope to get better at this as I get older, but time is running out. I would like to notice—a little earlier and with a little more certainty—what God is up to in my life and in my church. I would like to see God at work in this multiracial, multiethnic, multicultural congregation, bringing people together, helping us to recognize that our differences are not as large as we sometimes think they are.

I have a great deal of work to do. But I have a stubborn hope.

CHAPTER FIVE

Seek to Understand—
as Well as to Be Understood

Everyone at my church speaks English, more or less. You would think that this makes communication easier. And it does, to a point.

Most church members, as well as their children, speak several languages other than English, but English is the language we have agreed to use in worship and in every other area of church life. Our website proudly proclaims that we serve "the English-speaking community in Zürich and surrounding areas." And we do.

So, even though our members come from all over the world, we understand each other. We can talk together about our faith and our families and all the other things that are important to us, all because we have this common language, right?

Well, not quite. As it turns out, having a common language does not always mean that we understand each other. We try hard, but we often have our misunderstandings—sometimes humorous, sometimes not. It turns out that words and phrases which have plain meanings in one culture can mean something completely different in another culture.

A few weeks after my arrival, I was feeling pretty good about how things were going. The first weeks and months for a new pastor are critically important for the ministry that follows, and my start seemed to be very promising.

One Saturday morning I was putting the finishing touches on a sermon I planned to preach the next day. I have always enjoyed this final stage of sermon preparation. It's often the stage when I realize I have something worth saying, and for that reason it has become a cherished Saturday morning ritual.

What happened on this particular Saturday morning was that, instead of celebrating the masterpiece of a sermon I had created, I broke out in a cold sweat. I suddenly realized how idiomatic my spoken English is—and how difficult it must be for my congregation to understand.

"No one," I thought, slowly sinking into depression, "is going to understand what in the world I'm talking about."

An idiom, of course, is a phrase or an expression in which the words together have a meaning that's different from the dictionary definition of the individual words, and the English language is filled with them—idioms, that is. I read somewhere that the English language has nearly 4,000 relatively common idioms, and "to make a long story short" (there's one), anyone who wants to become fluent in English should be familiar with all or most of them.

"In the heat of the moment" (there's another), I reviewed my sermon and found that I had liberally sprinkled the sermon with lots of idioms that I happen to like and that make my sermons sound colorful and interesting—at least for the U.S. congregations I have served. But in order to be understood in my new context, I decided that I had to get rid of them, all of them, which isn't as easy as it sounds. I needed to "go back to the drawing board" (that's the last one, I promise).

Communication in a multicultural setting like my church requires a great deal of effort—far more than you might imagine. What one group of people hears and understands is not necessarily what another group of people hears and understands. I find myself in conversation with a nonnative speaker of English, and then to be sure I've spoken clearly, I will often end with, "Do you understand what I mean? Does that make sense to you?"

To be polite, most people say yes, but sometimes I wonder if they are being truthful.

Seek first to understand

But learning to speak more clearly is hardly the most important tool for leading or being a part of a multicultural church. Based on my experience I would say that learning to listen, really listen, is actually far more important.

I thought I was a good listener before I came to Switzerland. I have had some training, after all, and I have worked at it over the years.

A few summers ago I attended a week-long, intensive training event for church leaders who wanted to engage in a well-known listening and caring ministry, and early in the week I realized that my abilities in this area were sadly underdeveloped.

I had to admit that I don't really listen. Like most people I pretend to listen and I feign interest, but while another person is speaking I often think about what I want to say next. Or I'm thinking about whether I agree or disagree with what I am hearing. Or I'm thinking about the sort of advice I should give, because after all who isn't hoping for a precious nugget of wisdom from me?

Listening, I learned, requires discipline and practice, lots of it. But listening is more than patiently waiting for one's turn to speak. Careful listening requires concentration and the desire to understand what another person is saying—not simply the words being spoken, but the underlying feeling. A careful listener adopts a "caring, not curing" attitude to people who are speaking.

"Caring, not curing." That has been a tough one to master.

But—oh my—being listened to, knowing that I have been understood by another, feeling the deep pleasure of being understood is such a wonderful gift. It can be a moment of grace. And having received the gift myself, not once but several times, I came away from the training event determined to do my best to share it.

The late Stephen R. Covey, in his book *The 7 Habits of Highly Effective People: Restoring the Character Ethic*, writes that "we typically seek first to be understood. Most people do not listen with the intent to understand; they listen with the intent to reply. They're either speaking or preparing to speak. They're filtering everything through their own paradigms, reading their autobiography into other people's lives."

Covey challenges "highly effective people" to be better listeners, to seek to understand.

In a multicultural church context, careful listening, seeking to understand, and paying attention are critically important. Learning to listen may in fact be the first rule in multicultural communication— seeking to understand, paying attention to what is being said. This kind of communication can be painfully slow. We often want to move on to other business too quickly. But when we do, we can miss something of critical importance.

At a church board meeting soon after my arrival in Switzerland there was a discussion about interns. The church has had a strong history of interns coming from U.S. seminaries to spend a year learning ministry and enriching church life. Longtime church members remember each intern fondly. I was enthusiastic about continuing this tradition, and I volunteered to make contact with U.S. seminaries.

During the discussion, one of the elders (who is not from the U.S.) noted that U.S. seminary students had many more opportunities than, say, seminary students from Eastern Europe. Shouldn't we give other students this opportunity?

What was said and what I heard in this situation were, unfortunately, two different things. If I had listened more carefully, instead of rushing to judgment, I might have saved myself from embarrassment and everyone else some precious time.

What I heard, among other things, was that U.S. seminary students were "privileged." That word was never spoken, but that was the word I heard and therefore that was the word I responded to. I am defensive on this point, and therefore I reacted in what could be characterized as a "not-very-constructive manner." I gave a lengthy defense of U.S. seminary students and the enormous sacrifices they make and the student debt they carry with them into their first jobs and so on.

Everything I said was true, but my comments were not a direct response to what had been said. Most of the elders, to their credit, listened patiently until my irritation subsided. Later, when I was able to hear what was being said, we went on to have a more productive conversation about interns. And I had my first (but definitely not my last) lesson in cross-cultural conversation.

Kofi Annan, former Secretary-General of the United Nations, who has had a fair amount of experience in this area, who probably had to force himself a number of times to listen when he wanted to speak, has said, "Tolerance, inter-cultural dialogue, and respect for diversity are more essential than ever in a world where people are becoming more and more closely interconnected."

And when people are as "closely interconnected" as they are in a multicultural church, when people are trying with passion and conviction to live out the Christian faith together, communication skills—speaking and listening—are indispensable. But all of that, as Annan seems to say, is just the beginning point, the necessary first step.

The dominant and secondary culture issue

In nearly every multicultural setting, and certainly in every multicultural *church* setting, there will more than likely be a dominant culture and one or more secondary cultures or subcultures—in other words, one culture that exerts control and influence over the other cultures. Sometimes the dominant culture exerts more influence simply because it is the majority culture. Other times the dominant culture does not have a majority of the members, but it nevertheless has certain advantages, sometimes an economic advantage. (One version of the golden rule applies here: "Those who have the gold make the rules.")

Dominant cultures exert their influence by shaping the values and social norms for the entire group. This is true for businesses, universities, churches, and even countries. In the U.S. the dominant culture is English-speaking, has a Protestant Christian faith, and celebrates a European ancestry. Never mind that in the U.S. this dominant culture is no longer the majority culture—or is in the process of losing its majority culture status. The dominance of this culture continues to be pervasive and is likely to be pervasive for some time to come.

Those in the dominant culture are frequently not aware of or even sensitive to the control they exert, but their control is nevertheless pervasive, extending to every area of life. In the case of the church I serve, the dominant culture has determined language, dress, worship style, theological tradition, constitutional process, methods of conflict resolution, and a great deal more.

By adopting English as our language, for example, we have adopted what is essentially an egalitarian understanding of church life. Equality in social interactions is a fundamental assumption. English—unlike German and a few other languages—makes no distinction between formal and informal address. And in a theological tradition where the "priesthood of all believers" is already an important value, this egalitarian perspective has become deeply entrenched within church life.

But not all Asian, African, or South American cultures assume this same sort of egalitarian perspective. Some people within my church seem to feel more comfortable with clear social hierarchies. I can sense it in the way they shake my hand at the door. My easygoing "Hey, call me Doug" familiarity with everyone I meet—a deeply American trait—may be engaging for some, but it can be unsettling for others. Sometimes people who are not from the dominant culture are not sure what to do or say in those situations.

Becoming aware of the existence of a dominant culture, I have found, is one key to getting along with each other and learning to be tolerant. But even "becoming aware" is not enough. Once those in the dominant culture become aware of their power and influence—or have that power and influence pointed out to them—the response often ranges from denial ("You're exaggerating") to belligerence ("If they don't like it, they can leave") to self-pity ("Well, we're just doing our best"). Not everyone is ready right away to make use of the information.

At the International Protestant Church of Zürich, we seldom talk about dominant and secondary cultures. It is not a part of our vocabulary, and there is no reference to the matter on the website or in printed material. I think it's understood that American or western culture still exerts an influence on the church that is out of proportion to the number of U.S. citizens in the membership. I may be wrong about this, and my position within the dominant culture certainly affects my perspective, but—for much of the church's history—the dominant culture has mostly been an asset, mostly a positive thing.

I find myself at this point wanting to argue that the church thrives *precisely because* of this arrangement, and maybe at times it has, but the truth is that this situation is largely unexamined and unchallenged. We have a dominant culture—American or Western—and so far no one has thought to think much about it.

Still, the existence of a dominant culture at the very least demands awareness—not apology, maybe, but a recognition that such a thing exists, that it's real, that it's a powerful factor in church life. It's hard to imagine a healthy multicultural church without a healthy understanding of its cultural origins, expectations, and norms.

But it's not simply the willingness to recognize a dominant culture that is important for the health of a multicultural church. The secondary cultures within the church also need to be recognized and valued. The temptation is strong to absorb and assimilate them, or to cause them to bend to the will of the dominant culture.

A healthy, thriving multicultural church, however, will find a way to attend to the needs and hopes of its various secondary cultures. I have no data or polling to back up this claim. I suppose it's possible to find a thriving multicultural church that doesn't really care about its various secondary cultures. But that seems highly unlikely, doesn't it? In what is essentially a voluntary association, a secondary culture that is neglected or badly treated would most likely revolt or simply disappear.

Models for the multicultural church

All multicultural churches are not alike. Multicultural churches become multicultural churches in different ways. In my reading I have found several models of multicultural churches, as they exist today in the U.S., and these models illustrate both the hope and the inevitable conflict inherent in any multicultural church.

This is hardly a complete list, but I suspect that this list will include most multicultural churches in the world today.

1. Bi-cultural congregations. In this model for the multicultural church, there are two distinct racial or ethnic groups, comprising the majority of the membership. I am familiar with churches that have this model, and I am aware that this model presents significant challenges. Instead of one dominant culture and one secondary culture, both cultures exert considerable influence within the same congregation.

2. Congregations with a majority culture and significant influence from other cultures. I can imagine that this model would also present some significant challenges, and I suppose that this model is where many congregations in the U.S. begin the evolution to becoming a multicultural church. The key, of course, lies in the phrase "significant influence." A majority culture, especially if it has enjoyed exclusive or near-exclusive control over congregational life, would most likely have great difficulty letting go of its influence and privilege, and in both subtle and overt ways will fight to maintain it. It's difficult to imagine, except under extraordinary circumstances or perhaps with

extraordinary leadership, that a majority culture would simply let go of its control or dominance. A church that is intentional about becoming more culturally diverse, however, will make some deliberate and perhaps painful choices. Critically important will be attempts to become more diverse in leadership, an issue I address in another chapter.

3. Congregations with no single cultural majority. The congregation I currently serve fits this model, and it's difficult to imagine that many congregations in the U.S. can claim to have it. In worship at IPC on any given Sunday, there are more than two dozen nationalities represented, with no single nationality in a majority. I am aware that this phenomenon is typical of the international church. And though this model may look easy, especially to the church that is just setting off on the path to becoming multicultural, I can assure you that it is not. Beyond that, as I have described, there is clearly a dominant culture at IPC, even though that culture is not (and most likely never was) a majority culture. That dominant culture continues to exert influence at every level.

4. Nesting churches that provide homes for congregations of different cultures. I served a mostly white, Anglo church in Michigan several years ago that made space available to a Taiwanese congregation. Too often, I confess, we thought that "making space available" was the extent of our relationship, making the Taiwanese congregation incidental to the larger congregation. We were happiest when the nesting congregation stayed out of our way. To use the language of this chapter, the dominant culture often thought of the secondary culture as little more than "renters" and often as a nuisance. Slowly, though, the two congregations began to look for ways to integrate their two ministries—and their two congregations. The "nesting" model is often a good model for ethnic congregations who are unable to afford meeting space, but moving beyond the category of landlord and tenant, I can say from experience, is extraordinarily challenging. Strong leadership would seem to be required.

5. New churches beginning—intentionally—as multicultural congregations. Maybe most new churches, especially those in cities and urban areas, will now begin this way. This model seems to have significant advantages—and perhaps it does—but it also has some predictable challenges. As I have noted, a decision as basic as choosing a language for worship will have unintended consequences throughout church life.

6. Churches being redeveloped in changing neighborhoods. This model is similar to #2, but in this model the majority-culture congregation held on for a long time before decisions about the future had to be made. Many existing churches start down the path to becoming multicultural because their neighborhoods have changed around them. When the church was first started, there was a dominant culture in the neighborhood or community, and over time that culture changed, but not within the church. Not all churches feel called to make this change. Many of them closed or moved. But some—rather heroically—hear this call and make the necessary changes.

The point I want to make with this listing is that there is no single model, no right way, to become a multicultural church. What seems to be more important than the model is the intention or the desire to be multicultural. As I have argued in a previous chapter, that remains the key.

A long, and not always distinguished, track record

The Christian church may seem like an unusual place to look to for cultural sensitivity and healthy cross-cultural relationships.

Anyone who has read James Michener's *Hawaii* or has seen a movie like *Mosquito Coast* is likely to think of the influence of the church as destructive, incapable of much cultural sensitivity. As Michener depicted the missionary movement to Hawaii, the unspoiled indigenous culture was overrun by boorish Western missionaries who were intolerant of the "heathen" gods and the "savage" customs of the people they found. In addition to Christian faith, the missionaries brought disease, intolerance, and eventually capitalism. Until recently, missionaries were often condemned as exporters of American civilization first and Christian faith second.

More recent treatments of the nineteenth-century missionary movement have been more nuanced and much more charitable. It seems likely that some of these early missionary efforts were indeed fueled by racist assumptions and dominant culture superiority, but what also seems likely is that these Christian missionaries were among the first to try to understand and engage other cultures. The Wycliffe Bible translators, to give one small example, have now translated the entire Bible into 531 languages and the New Testament into a total of 1,329 languages (the numbers are from their own website). In the process, Wycliffe has played a major role in linguistic development and language preservation. More than a few cultures around the world might have disappeared altogether were it not for the work of Wycliffe and others.

Whatever the criticisms of the missionary movement, and however justified those criticisms might be, the underlying impulse of the Christian faith is to "go therefore and make disciples of all nations." This missionary impulse has brought Christian faith to nearly every country on the planet. Some of this work has been so successful, in fact, that some of these countries are now returning the favor by sending missionaries back to the countries where the missionary movement originated.

The result of this powerful missionary impulse is that Christians generally and the church specifically have been doing the work of engaging with other cultures for a long, long time.

Peter and Cornelius

The description of the early church in the book of Acts contains a surprising number of conflicts, many of them cultural in nature. Anyone who thinks that the church, which had its start at Pentecost, expanded smoothly and continuously until it reached Rome should reread the book, especially the early chapters. A number of critically important issues had to be sorted out. The big one, of course, concerned Gentiles and what to do with them.

This is how a dominant culture thinks: Secondary cultures are often problems to be managed.

The dominant culture in the earliest days of the church—Jewish Christians—found themselves with a new and unexpected secondary culture: Gentile Christians. Acts tells several stories, but it certainly tells the story of how a dominant culture slowly, often with great reluctance, came to grips with the existence of a growing secondary culture. One Lord, one faith, one baptism, yes, but two totally different worldviews.

It was the apostle Paul, more than anyone else, who brought the good news of Jesus' death and resurrection to Gentiles around the eastern Mediterranean world and who will always be remembered as the church's greatest missionary, but Acts makes clear that it was the apostle Peter who made Paul's work possible. I suppose one could argue that only someone with Peter's stature within the early church, someone who had been a close friend and confidant of Jesus, could have made this change happen.

Based on what we know, Peter was a good Jew. He had undoubtedly been brought up to understand the proper relationship between Jews and Gentiles. In the Jewish worldview, Gentiles did not even have the status of a secondary culture; they were something other and therefore to be avoided. When Jesus told his disciples to "go therefore and make disciples of all nations" (Matt. 28:19), it's not clear what *they* heard, but it was most likely not what *we* hear in those words.

For much of his life, Peter wrestled with the truth that Gentiles counted as equals before God (Gal. 2:11–14), that the gospel really was for all people, Jews and Gentiles alike.

One afternoon, not long after Pentecost (Acts 10), Peter went to his rooftop to pray and saw the famous vision of a sheet being lowered to the ground by its four corners. On the sheet, we are told, were "all kinds of four-footed creatures and reptiles and birds of the air." The voice accompanying the vision said, "Get up, Peter, kill and eat," a command that had to have been puzzling and even disturbing. Peter was raised not to eat such animals.

Peter protested, as any first-century Jew would have: "By no means, Lord: for I have never eaten anything that is profane or unclean."

But the instruction was repeated to Peter two more times. Before he had time to grasp the meaning of the vision, Peter was on his way to Caesarea where Cornelius, the Roman centurion, was waiting for him. This was not to be a private meeting, however; with Cornelius were his "relatives and close friends," all of them Gentiles.

Peter seems to speak reluctantly throughout the story. This meeting, after all, was not his idea. He is plainly uncomfortable about being in Cornelius's home. But, give him credit, he presses on. And while he "was still speaking," the Holy Spirit fell upon all who heard Peter speak. And then Peter did the only thing he could imagine doing in this situation. He baptized everyone in the name of Jesus. Not because it was his idea, of course, but because the circumstances demanded it, the Spirit demanded it. This became his defense when Jewish Christians, members of the dominant culture, "criticized" his behavior (Acts 11:2). "Who was I that I could hinder God?" he said (Acts 11:17).

It's fair to say that what happened in Cornelius's residence that day had far-reaching implications that even Peter did not understand for a long time.

I have reflected on that story from Acts 10 many times over the years, but never while serving a multicultural church. Like most Bible stories, the story about Peter and Cornelius works at several different levels. What has always seemed clear to me is that Peter did not know—and could not have known—what God was up to. Having been raised in the dominant culture, having been thoroughly schooled in the habits and biases of that culture, Peter could not have acted in any other way. That he followed God's leading at all is a tribute to his sincere desire to be faithful.

A member of the dominant culture

Here is something about the story I had never considered before: the secondary culture described throughout the book of Acts was about to become—perhaps within Peter's own lifetime—the majority culture and soon thereafter the dominant culture. The church was well on its way to becoming a predominantly Gentile Christian church, with Jewish Christians slowly taking on the role of a minority culture (and then all but disappearing).

As a member of the dominant culture in my church—as the leader and representative of that culture!—I sometimes wonder what this story means for me. I probably make the interpretation more difficult than it should be, but I do not always see what I am supposed to see.

In the course of my work, I find myself in Cornelius's household nearly every day. I am surrounded by his relatives and friends. These are people I might not have chosen as friends. In many ways, in spite of my best efforts, they are strangers to me. Like most American Christians, I have tended to stay with what I know and what is most familiar. These are good and loving people, but they are not members of the group I know best. So, in Cornelius's household I am anxious. Like Peter, I measure my words. I smile politely, but I am always worried about making a mistake and saying the wrong thing.

Members of my church's secondary cultures are unfailingly respectful of my dominant culture status. I sometimes wish they weren't quite as respectful as they are. Their respect is awkward for me. They insist on calling me "pastor," for example, and not "Doug." It is an honor for them to have me eat with them in their homes. I would often prefer to stay home, but my presence in their homes means more than I sometimes realize. I am startled that by entering their homes I bring far more with me than my appetite.

But my membership in the dominant culture, I have come to see, is hardly their first concern. Their first concern is to know God. They are eager to have a relationship with this God. They long to worship this

God. When the time is right, they would like to be baptized. They treat me with respect mostly because it is this other thing that they most desire. I am like Peter in that way. It is not my culture or my status within that culture that interests them so much as what I can tell them about Jesus.

I am the one who feels awkward and frightened. But apparently not awkward and frightened enough to do much about it. I am not proud of this, but I find that I almost always work to preserve the status of the dominant culture. I try to be more aware of this, but the habits and biases are deeply ingrained. I have lived so long in the dominant culture—first in the U.S. and now here—that I find I cannot help myself. Perhaps this is always the first concern of a dominant culture. Not what God might be doing in any given situation, but instead how to preserve what I have always known and found comfortable, what feels like my right.

The good news is that God's purposes were accomplished in spite of Peter's reluctance. Perhaps the good news in Zürich will be something similar. God's will, not mine, will be done.

See translation desk

Recently, while looking for something else, I came across a website for a church in Brisbane, Australia (Queensland), called the International City Church, and I was astonished by the extraordinary effort this congregation is making to provide a church home to many different language groups and nationalities. I have never been to this church, but someday I would like to go there and see their ministry for myself. One of my church members from Australia has confirmed that the experience would not disappoint.

The church has Sunday morning worship at nine and eleven, which is not at all unusual, but it was the note below worship times that caught my attention: "Both services will be in English with Chinese (Mandarin) & Spanish translations available. Translations into Korean, Cantonese,

& some other languages may be available upon request—see translation desk."

As a pastor I think about the level of organization, coordination, and financial commitment all of this must require. I'm fairly certain a paid staff member would have to be assigned and volunteers trained.

Perhaps members of this Brisbane church would respond as members in U.S. churches did to the statement "our church is doing enough to be ethnically diverse," but I doubt it. They have clearly made it their mission to reach as many language groups as possible, to be understood as well as to understand.

And I suppose that is the key—not only the intention, but the *commitment* to make sure all are welcome.

IPC does not have a translation desk or any translation services. We consider it a good day when the sound system performs as it is supposed to. I find myself just a little envious. I wish we had a translation desk, but I don't think we will have one for the foreseeable future. And yet, there is something wonderful about the idea.

All multicultural churches, I think, should have a translation desk—the kind that International City Church has, possibly, but also the other kind, what we might call the spiritual kind. I can imagine a church where people are doing their best to listen and to make sense of what others are saying. I can imagine a church that commits both time and resources to this work. No electronic gadgets, but hearts that are attuned to all.

Wasn't this the surprise of Pentecost? "Amazed and astonished," the story tells us in Acts 2, the gathered crowd asked aloud, "How is it that we hear, each of us, in our own native language?" I hear delight in that statement, as well as surprise. We aren't used to someone taking the time or making the effort to communicate in such a way that we understand and that we feel wanted.

It would be as if I said, "I don't understand," and the person who heard me said, "We will do whatever it takes, we will spend whatever is necessary, because you are that important to us."

And to that I would say, "At last I have found my church home."

CHAPTER SIX

Learn the Language

How can I put this delicately? I can't, so I'll put it bluntly: Americans are lazy when it comes to language learning. So lazy, in fact, that 75 percent of Americans speak only their mother tongue, with no second language, according to a recent YouGov.com survey.

You would think that this language laziness would be a source of em-barrassment—or least enough of an incentive to learn a language other than English, or maybe an incentive to insist that our children learn a second language while they are still young enough to achieve fluency. But you would be wrong. Forty-three percent of Americans will say, when surveyed, that it's important to learn another language, but that means the majority do not see the value of it, and in fact many Americans are strongly *opposed* to the idea.

When presidential candidate Barack Obama suggested during his campaign in 2008 that language learning should be a priority, and that Spanish would be a good second language for Americans to learn, he was met with strong resistance. Some even suggested that he was planning to make Spanish the national language. His campaign quickly issued a clarification, and we have heard very little about the matter since then.

For the record, Obama is not fluent in a language other than English. And neither am I. But that doesn't change my belief—or Obama's, I suspect—that language learning is a good idea. And not only do I believe that language learning is a good idea, but I also believe that learning to speak the languages of the people in our congregations—and the communities in which those congregations are found—will make our churches stronger and better able to carry out our most essential mission, which is to tell others the good news.

Language learning should no longer be treated as nice but not necessary. Churches, especially their pastors, need to rethink their attitudes to language learning. We could be the leaders in this, and we would have good biblical and theological reasons for doing so, which I will get to in this chapter, but as with too many other matters we are often the followers.

In the interest of full disclosure

As I mentioned earlier, the church I serve in Switzerland is an English-speaking congregation. Weekly worship is in English, I preach and lead worship in English, and all of our publications and meetings and classes are in English. If you were to navigate to my church's website, you would find that it too is in English. I was selected to be pastor, at least in part, because I (sometimes) communicate well in English.

So, why devote an entire chapter to the importance of language learning when I seem to be getting along just fine in my native English? I suppose that the pastor of every North American church would ask the same question: Is language learning really necessary?

I am fluent in only one language—English—and some days I wonder about my abilities in that one. English novelist George Orwell once wrote that "in my life I have learned seven foreign languages, including two dead ones, and out of those seven I retain only one, and that not brilliantly." I know a little of how he felt.

Mastering one language is hard work. But a second? Or a third?

In high school, which was my earliest opportunity to learn a language other than English, I chose Latin. I no longer remember why. My parents seemed pleased, though, and others were impressed when I told them. So, I continued with Latin for three years in high school and even added another year of it in college.

The thing is, few people speak Latin anymore, and after all of the time I spent learning it, I don't use it. The best result of my Latin studies, as far as I can tell, is that I finally grasped English grammar. Something about learning Latin solved the riddle that the English language had always been for me. I could finally distinguish between direct and indirect objects. So there's that.

Now, I find myself in a country where most people seem to speak at least English, even though the four *official* languages of Switzerland—German, French, Italian, and Romansch—do not include English. When you ask a Swiss if he or she speaks English, the answer is invariably "a little," though that person then proceeds to speak to you in flawless, often unaccented English.

To blow your mind about the language-learning skills in this country, the Swiss where I live don't really like to speak German; they prefer to speak *Schwyzerdütsch*—or Swiss German. Swiss German sounds as though it might be a dialect of German, but it's not, really. It's an entirely different language with the same root as German. At least that's what the Swiss will tell you.

Anyway, do the math here. The typical Swiss speaks *a lot* of languages—Swiss German, German, French, English, and often Italian. But that's just the beginning. That's what is entirely normal and expected for people who, in the U.S., would consider themselves to be "college educated." One of my elders, who speaks all of the languages I just mentioned, plus Dutch, has now, at age fifty, started to learn Spanish. Why? Because, he says, it might be useful in his business.

The typical U.S. response to this remarkable situation is that Switzerland is geographically small and surrounded by other countries, so of course the Swiss have no choice but to learn other languages. It's a matter of necessity.

And that is certainly true. But the point is, they do it. And they do it as well as any country in the world today, except perhaps for the Dutch, who are also striking in their language proficiency. Several years ago—it's hard to remember, but Switzerland was once quite a poor country—the Swiss decided that to be competitive in the world economy, to have a chance in the global marketplace, they would have to require their children to learn English. That decision (as well as a few others) has helped the Swiss develop one of the highest standards of living in the world, with one of the highest per-capita incomes in the world. And according to a recent United Nations World Happiness Report (2015), the Swiss are also among the happiest people in the world, out of 158 countries in the ranking. (The Swiss seem to trade the number-one position each year with Denmark or other Scandinavian countries.)

I can't make a direct link, of course, between language learning and happiness (or even the current Swiss standard of living). But recent research is beginning to show the remarkable benefits of language learning in other areas of life. People who learn a second language have better job prospects, a measurable cognitive boost, and even some protection against dementia.

When I moved to Switzerland, one of the requirements for my work permit was that I make steady progress toward language proficiency in German—not Swiss German, but *Hochdeutsch* or standard German, the native language of 90 to 95 million people on the planet (and as many as 175 to 220 million who know German as a second or foreign language).

Makes sense, doesn't it? Americans want immigrants to the U.S. to do the same, to learn English, the official language of their new country. (By the way, if I had moved to Geneva in the western part of Switzerland—the French-speaking part of the country—the requirement for my permit would have been that I learn French. The aim, as far as I can tell, is integration within the culture, not necessarily language proficiency.)

This rule is enforced by the office of integration issues (*der Kantonalen*

Fachstelle für Integrationsfragen), where I must report every year to Frau Marais, who is very nice and speaks flawless, unaccented English. I must provide evidence to her of my progress—which, to be honest, seems to me to be moving at a snail's pace.

Among other things, this annual appointment with Frau Marais is a lesson in humility and therefore provides a powerful incentive to keep going with my language studies. I have been competitive in all areas of my life, and that quality has been mostly helpful in this area as well.

Interestingly—and here is the reason for this long explanation of Swiss language habits—members of my congregation also seem very interested in my progress, very interested that I am making *any* progress, very interested that I am even making the *attempt* to learn one of their languages. It's not that they want to hear me preach in German next Sunday—*Nein!*—it's that they want to know of my commitment to learning their language, their culture, their history, their way of life. They value my commitment, and they see it as part of my interest, my *investment*, in them. If I failed to learn their language—and therefore, as they see it, their culture—would I truly be invested in them?

Why is it so hard for churches and church members in the U.S. to understand this simple truth? Nothing suggests indifference—and perhaps arrogance—so loudly as the unwillingness to learn, engage, and appreciate another culture, and nothing is quite so closely connected with a culture as its language.

From the first day, language learning for me has been about more than vocabulary and grammar. It has been about the way people think and interact with each other.

In my first or second week of language class, which I attended shortly after arriving in the country, the class learned about ordering food from the menu in restaurants—obviously a very helpful language skill to have. And my teacher, Frau Zopfi, mentioned that Germans ordinarily use the equivalent of "I will take" when they place an order, while Swiss ordinarily say, "I would, if it's possible, like to have."

To Frau Zopfi this subtle difference spoke volumes about the difference between Germans and Swiss. She might have added, "And now you can understand why we don't like Germans."

I have a dear friend in Switzerland who has lived in this country for 20 years and who speaks only English (the work permit for pastors and other religious workers comes with a different set of rules and higher expectations). That he has survived for so long without learning to speak German (or any of the other national languages) is a tribute to the welcoming spirit of the Swiss culture. That he has so far refused to "integrate"—the word that locals prefer to use in connection with foreigners living here— suggests that he is either arrogant, ignorant, or lazy. And yet, in my personal interactions with him, I do not find him to be any of those things. He has worked hard, for example, to establish a successful business in a foreign country. He is anything but ignorant or lazy.

So, is the failure to learn the language really a matter of arrogance?

I wish I could answer otherwise, but I have reluctantly come to the conclusion that the answer is yes. I have come to see that this is in fact a blind spot many Americans have. We have grown accustomed to having other cultures bend to our will, our way of doings, our language, and so at best we are out of practice when it comes to learning, engaging, understanding, and appreciating another culture. Don't get me wrong—there are many qualities in American culture to celebrate. But this is not one of them.

Makes sense, doesn't it?

One Sunday at a church I served in the U.S., I noticed a group of six or seven women talking together at the coffee hour after morning worship. What these women had in common, I knew, was that they were originally from South America and had married men from the U.S.—not a lot to have in common, not enough to form a support group, maybe, but it was something.

Their home countries included Peru, Chile, and one or two others. They were (and are) bright and well-educated. One of them is an attorney who specializes in immigration issues for a large Miami-based law firm. As I passed the group, I was intrigued to hear that they were speaking English with each other, even though the native language of each was Spanish.

As I thought about it further, I remembered that only one of their husbands had made an attempt to learn Spanish. He was also the only one of the husbands who regularly accompanied his wife on annual trips to see her family. He was far from fluent in her language, but he could understand her family members during those annual visits.

The rest of the husbands? Not a pretty picture, I'm afraid. I would often hear the husbands complain about having to make the trip with their wives, about the chore it was to spend time with the families. The husbands tried to sound generous by saying to their wives, "You can go any time you want. And take the kids!"

I suppose it had not occurred to them that one important way to be married is to know your partner as well as you possibly can, to show an interest in her life (and culture).

Churches, in my experience, exhibit a similar attitude to some of their members and to some of their surrounding communities. They try to be kind (in a paternalistic sort of way), indulgent (ditto), but not exactly engaged, not exactly curious, and not exactly loving.

I would like to think that if I had stayed longer in South Florida, where my previous church was located, I would have had to learn Spanish. The truth is, I should have started learning Spanish on my first day at that church. The search committee should have required either the language skill or the willingness to learn.

After English, Spanish is the second most-spoken language in the region. And in many neighborhoods it is the *most* spoken language. My church should have treated language learning as an expectation for me and for every member of the staff. How were we going to reach the people in our community with the good news of the gospel if we didn't learn to speak their language, if we showed no interest whatsoever in their culture?

The response, never verbalized, but widely understood, was that we would wait for everyone else to learn our language and our culture.

And then, of course, we wondered why we were not a multicultural church.

Within the last few months, my church in Switzerland commissioned a young couple and their daughter for mission service in Thailand. They are planning to live and work among the poor in Chiang Mai, one of the larger cities in the north of the country where a large number of Shan live.

The Shan are a large ethnic group in southeast Asia, and like many such groups they have their own language. It is similar to Thai in that it is also a tonal language, but it is very much a distinct and separate language. Tonal languages are common in Asia and are often extremely difficult for Westerners to learn. The meaning of a word, for example, can change depending on which syllable is emphasized. The mission organization that is sponsoring this couple is requiring that they learn the language of the Shan. The first year—at least—of their mission will be spent in language school.

Seems reasonable to me. Doesn't it to you? And the couple, as far as I can tell, seem to be embracing the challenge with excitement and determination, two qualities that are necessary (but, alas, not sufficient) for later-in-life language learning. Caring for the poor in northern Thailand, working in a clinic for HIV-infected people, engaging people who live in remote villages—to do all of that we would expect that missionaries would learn to speak the language, wouldn't we?

Why is it, then, that the church in the United States is so slow to catch on to this way of thinking, to require the same skills of our own pastors that we would require of our missionaries? I don't know the answer to the question, but I do know that it is an important question to ask.

Not only that, but it's biblical

I think it is important to ground this appeal biblically. In Leviticus 19:34 we find the words "the foreigner residing among you must be treated as your native-born. Love them as yourself, for you were foreigners in

Egypt." This is not an isolated theme in Scripture. The logic seems to be that "you know what it's like to have been a foreigner, so treat the foreigner as you yourself would have wanted to be treated in Egypt."

David I. Smith, a member of the faculty at Calvin College in Grand Rapids, Michigan, has made the case in a couple of books—especially *Learning from the Stranger: Christian Faith and Cultural Diversity*—and across a number of years that language learning is essential to the work that Christians are called to do. He argues that the willingness to learn another's language and to go through the effort and persistence needed to speak to another person in the way that resonates with *their* heart, being willing to listen to and learn from *their* stories, is one form that this commitment to being there for others can take.

I like the way that former South African president Nelson Mandela is said to have expressed it, after he spent long years learning to speak Afrikaans, the language of those responsible for his 27 years of imprisonment: "If you talk to a man in a language he understands, that goes to his head. If you talk to him in his language, that goes to his heart."

Not only the Old Testament, but also the New Testament could be cited here. In Matthew 7:12 (where Jesus seems to be drawing explicitly on Leviticus 19), Jesus says, "Do to others what you would have them do to you." The foreigner, while we were looking the other way, has become our neighbor. The foreigner has moved in next door or down the block.

Obviously language learning is only one behavior that might be suggested by Jesus' words, but (as Smith points out), it's worth pondering what most English speakers would like others to do for them. I think I know. The English speakers I observe in my travels around the world *expect* that others will speak to them in English.

I feel convicted by Smith's argument: Loving others as oneself, he says, implies listening to them, understanding their hopes and needs, "according to them their full humanity" (as he puts it), and seeking their well-being even at my own expense.

If I had heard that sort of reasoning earlier in my life, that appeal to my faith and what it asks of me, I wonder if I would have waited so long to learn a second language.

Humility

One good by-product of language learning, I've discovered, is humility. I am using the word "good" here in the same way I would say that a vegetable like kale is good for me. I thought I was humble enough before I started my language learning, but now I realize that there are several deeper layers of humility I needed to explore.

Language learning has been "good" for me in that sense.

I was a late, late bloomer in school, but at some point during my adolescence I started to do well. Maybe it was just the rampant grade inflation at the time, but I received (and started to expect) good grades. And so, what now seems clear is that I was very overconfident when I arrived in Switzerland and took my first German language class.

My 90-minute evening classes are taught entirely in German, and I find myself most weeks struggling to keep up. I look around and think, "What did she say?" And in that way, I have become a slow learner again. My teacher, Frau Zopfi, is encouraging, of course, as she is for the one or two other slow learners in my class, but I can clearly see (and hear) the difference in my progress and that of others.

During a week-long, summer intensive class at the Goethe Institut in Berlin, my teacher there, Frau Proksch, tried to encourage me by saying that my "German needed more melody." (She and I both knew that my German needs more than that.)

Anyway, my experience with an international church has allowed me to see that learning a language (and learning the humility that goes with it) are unusually good ways to appreciate the difficult transitions faced by other immigrant groups who live in our neighborhoods and communities. I am now acutely aware of what other people I have known over the years have had to do to move to the U.S., to feel comfortable in conversation with me, to accomplish the most basic of daily tasks such as going to the grocery store and dropping off the dry cleaning and getting a haircut.

One earlier challenge I ignored

I have been preaching long enough to know how to get a laugh, and laughter can sometimes be an effective tool of communication. I try to use the tool sparingly, but some stories and anecdotes are too good not to tell. I usually know when I've got a good one.

One Sunday I told a story about preaching at a small church in Haiti. The church I was serving at the time had a significant mission presence in Haiti, and I had the opportunity to travel often to Haiti and be a part of this work. On one such trip I was asked to preach in a small Episcopal church located in a rural area.

The language of Haiti is Creole, and I know only a few words of Creole, but the priest assured me that he would provide a simultaneous translation of my sermon. I would speak a sentence or two in English, and he would translate, on the spot, into Creole. What was humorous about my anecdote was that I would sometimes speak a sentence, and the Haitian priest seemed to go on for several minutes. And then other times I would speak a sentence, and he would look at me as if to say, "I've already covered that."

When I finished my sermon, I told my congregation, I had no idea what that Haitian church actually heard.

The story received a big laugh from my congregation, as I knew it would. For some reason, Americans love travel stories involving misunderstandings and miscommunications. Part of the humor, I suppose, is that we always sound slightly superior, even when we seem to be poking fun at ourselves.

When worship was over—not in Haiti, but at the church in the U.S. where I told the story—a relatively new member of the church approached me, and I could see that he was not amused by my sermon. The church member, ironically enough, had just immigrated from Switzerland (long before I imagined moving there myself) to take a teaching position at the University of Michigan. He looked at me and said, in flawless English, "Doug, that story was not funny. It's time for you to learn to speak the language of the people you're preaching to. And if it's not Creole, then pick another. But do it."

And almost immediately I felt convicted. I knew he was right. But at the time I did nothing about it.

I should mention in this connection that I have taken classes in biblical Hebrew and Greek. I grew up in one of the few American denominations that still requires its pastors to have a working knowledge of biblical languages, and so my seminary years were filled with language learning—not, alas, learning to listen to and speak another language, but learning to read.

I thought I knew my Bible well when I arrived at seminary, but learning the languages in which the books of the Bible were originally written was an unexpected delight. A new world opened up. I heard the stories in a new and more profound way. I will never read John's Gospel again, for example, without seeing all of the rich vocabulary there, the layers of meaning that suddenly became visible.

Do I understand how learning a language might deepen my life and faith? Yes.

Speaking the language of your people

There's another dimension to language learning that I want to explore.

This may sound odd at first, but I have had to learn a new language each time I moved to a new church. Moving from one congregation to another requires learning the *spiritual* language of the new congregation. Even when moving from one Presbyterian church to another, from one church in the Midwest to another, there is a change of language. Sometimes the change is subtle, but surprisingly it is often profound.

When I moved, several years ago, from a Presbyterian church in Wheaton, Illinois, to another Presbyterian church—this one in Ann Arbor, Michigan—I realized that the adjustment was far greater than I anticipated. And the single biggest part of that adjustment was in the spiritual language I needed to learn.

In Wheaton, many of my members worked in downtown Chicago. They commuted by train each day. They knew the business world. They either worked for the equities markets in Chicago or were closely connected to them. There were also more lawyers in that Wheaton church than I had ever found in one church before.

And so, to learn to speak their language, I found myself reading the *Wall Street Journal*. It was delivered to my home. I made a conscious choice to subscribe. I didn't always agree—okay, I *seldom* agreed—with the political point of view, but I learned a new vocabulary, a new way of looking at the world. Because I knew the language of my people, I could speak to them in what I thought was an effective manner. I can remember several key moments in the history of that church when it was critically important to know their language.

A special prayer service on the evening of September 11, 2001, was one such key moment, but there were others. In moments of profound crisis or trauma, sometimes the only language that speaks to us, that comforts us, that offers meaning and hope is our native language. I remember the prayer service that evening, and what I remember was finding in my own pain the words church members most needed to hear.

As it turns out, I was not alone. Lots of other pastors were working just as hard. Some of the finest sermons ever preached in the English language were preached that night, or in the days immediately following. Many of them have found their way into sermon collections.

But then, not long after, I moved—not far in terms of miles, but a continent away in terms of spiritual language. In Ann Arbor, Michigan, many members of my church were connected in some way to the University of Michigan. They viewed the world, typically, not with the eyes of business, but with the eyes of academia. Let's just say that a university town is vastly different, in some important ways, from the bedroom community of a major city.

Soon after I moved, I read somewhere that the *New York Times* had its second-highest concentration of readers in, of all places, Ann Arbor. Without giving the matter much thought at the time, I started to have the *New York Times* delivered to my home. Both the *Journal* and the *Times* are exceptionally well-written newspapers, but each has a different worldview, which may be the understatement of this chapter. But to be an effective pastor and preacher in my new setting, I believed that I needed to understand this other worldview. To use the language of this chapter, I believed that I needed to speak the *spiritual* language of my congregation—and to do so as soon as possible.

Learning to speak the spiritual language of my current congregation in Zürich, Switzerland, has proved to be even more of a challenge. Okay, *that* is the understatement of this chapter. I wish that subscribing to a different newspaper—the *Neue Zürcher Zeitung*, for example—would have helped. The truth is, I had no idea how vastly different the spiritual language would be in this setting. No one could have prepared me.

True, we all speak English, some better than others. All (or almost all) of us believe in Jesus Christ as our Lord and Savior. We also believe that the Bible is in some way God's Word to us. But beyond those things, and maybe a few other points, we have little in common. The diversity is—how should I put it?—staggering. Each day, each meeting, each appointment in my office brings a new challenge to our communication and a new opportunity for misunderstanding.

An English-speaking, international church will attract Anglicans and Pentecostals and everything in between. It will provide a home to those who believe in baptizing babies and children, as well as those who think that only believers should be baptized. It will attract those who are accustomed to three-hour services with a minimum of one hour of preaching, as well as those who are accustomed to one-hour services and eighteen-minute sermons. It will have many varying views on leadership, both pastoral and lay. Beyond all of that, the members of an international church will have come to faith through the work of an astonishing variety of Christian pastors and teachers. Believers in India, to give one example, come to faith in a much different way from, say, believers in the U.K. What is emphasized in one culture is not necessarily emphasized in another. Even native English speakers will use different words to describe the same thing.

The degree of difficulty in learning to speak the spiritual language in an international church is very, very high, but I think the experience can be instructive for the North American church, which is becoming more diverse every day.

Our language of faith

I take language classes in the village where I live, called Meilen, which is a 15-minute train ride from the *Hauptbahnhof*, the main train station in Zürich. The language school is on the second floor of an office building, though it seems to have been an apartment building at one time. There is a kitchen, a restroom (*die Toilette*, an important word to know!), and three to four bedrooms, which are now classrooms with tables and dry-erase boards.

I learn my vocabulary and verb conjugations by sitting in these rooms each week and listening to Frau Zopfi speak a surprisingly pleasant German, but I learn the language by making my way around the village, buying groceries and speaking with my neighbors. I can sometimes fake my way through an evening German class, but I find that sitting in a barber's chair, for example, is what one might call the real world.

How hard can it be to say "shorter on the sides, longer on top"? As it turns out, plenty hard.

I went for a haircut last week, sat down in the chair, and my barber, who was in her early twenties, sized me up pretty quickly as an American. Everyone does. Very politely, and in excellent English, she said, "Would you like me to speak German or English?" It was a gracious offer.

"*Deutsch*," I answered, hoping to impress this young woman, who was younger than both of my daughters.

Our conversation did not get very far. She asked me where I was from—"*Woher kommen Sie?*"—and what I was doing in Switzerland.

I answered, "*Ich bin ein Pfarrer*," trying to tell her that I am a pastor. She said (in English), "You're a driver?"

This happens frequently. I speak plainly in the other person's *native* language, and the response is a puzzled look. What?

"*Pfarrer*," I said, a bit louder, as though volume was the main problem in our communication.

Turns out, the German for the words "pastor" and "driver" sound something alike, at least to a non-native speaker like me. I quickly told her that I was not a driver, at least not professionally. "I am a pastor," I say, this time in English.

"Oh," she said. As it turned out, her father was a pastor too. We had much to talk about.

In *The Innocents Abroad*, Mark Twain tells of a similar experience: "In Paris they just simply opened their eyes and stared when we spoke to them in French! We never did succeed in making those idiots understand their own language."

Sometimes I feel the same way. "I'm speaking *your* language, for heaven's sake. Why is it that you can't understand me?"

I have felt this way over the years while preaching too—preaching English to an English-speaking congregation. "I am a native speaker," I think, "and yet you still do not understand me?"

I even try speaking louder in the pulpit, sometimes shouting, as though that might help, but it is not that they cannot hear me. It is that I have not found the words to communicate the truths I want them to hear, the truths to which I have devoted my life.

It is frustrating and humbling. At times I want to give up. And then ultimately I go back to my desk, to my laptop, to my Bible. My work, as it turns out, has always been to find the right words to say what I know to be true.

CHAPTER SEVEN

Move Beyond Cultural Stereotypes

Heaven is . . . where the police are British,
the cooks are Italian,
the mechanics are German,
the lovers are French,
and it is all organized by the Swiss.

Hell is . . . where the police are German,
the cooks are English,
the mechanics are French,
the lovers are Swiss,
and it is all organized by the Italians.

Do you like that one? It's fun, isn't it? I have a lot more just like it. What I've learned, though, is that cultural stereotyping is fun—until it isn't.

Soon after my arrival in Switzerland, the church's youth group planned a special evening where I could get to know them and they could get to know me. After a few "get to know you" games, we divided into teams for a trivia contest. Someone thought it would be fun to divide up into four teams as follows: the Asians, the Africans, the Europeans, and the North Americans. The young man born in Paraguay suddenly (and reluctantly) found himself lumped together with the North Americans. Our lone Australian was assigned to the Asians.

The contest went as one might have expected. The Asians and the North Americans were very, very competitive. They were always leaning in. Their chairs kept getting closer to the person asking the trivia questions. Serious faces replaced smiling faces. Winning replaced having fun as the goal of the evening. Cheering and high-fiving erupted every time there was a correct answer.

The Africans, in contrast, hung back, not quite sure what to make of it all. Two of them—I became concerned about them—spent a great deal of time looking at their cell phones. And the others? They seemed bored.

What about the Europeans? Well, they observed everything with a cool detachment. They were the time-keepers, and they did it very efficiently. Since most of them were Swiss, they seemed at times more interested in making sure the rules were observed than in having any fun.

I went home that night not quite sure what to think of what had happened. One of the adult leaders assured me during the game that they had never divided into teams like this—based on continents and cultures. The comment sounded to me as though he was apologizing and admitting to a mistake.

Mostly the game was fun, mostly we were able to laugh at ourselves, but there were a few moments when I thought the evening was uncomfortable. As the game went on, I became increasingly aware that not everyone was enjoying the game as much as I was. I didn't realize it at the time, but I was getting my first lesson in cultural stereotyping, the first of many.

How my mind has changed

I wasn't so alarmed about cultural stereotyping, I confess, until I was the one being stereotyped. I am an American, but I don't think I realized how obvious my nationality was (and is) until I moved to Switzerland.

Most people here can guess where I am from within a few seconds. I smile, and most Swiss don't, not when meeting strangers. I wear khaki (or used to), and most Swiss don't. Ditto with shorts. I like to laugh loudly at jokes, and most Swiss think people who do that sound like horses. I address people I meet for the first time by their first names, and when I do, most Swiss feel compelled to explain to me the difference between formal and informal forms of address.

To the Swiss, I am a stereotypical American—loud, horsey, and a little too quick with a big, toothy smile. But the stereotyping did not stop with my nationality.

My church members sized me up pretty quickly, even before I arrived. As they saw it, my brief biography contained many warning signs. I was proud of my biography, and I still am, but they saw some things differently. And the result was that I felt hurt by all of the stereotypes that they applied to me.

I am Presbyterian, and to some that meant I was liberal and expected to be paid a lot of money.

I have a daughter who is also a Presbyterian pastor, and to some that meant I did not take the Bible's teachings about women seriously. (No one has yet said to me, "Isn't it wonderful that in adulthood your children have embraced the Christian faith?")

I practiced yoga briefly in the U.S., as I mentioned in the introduction, and for some that meant I had been influenced by Eastern religions and quite possibly evil spirits.

I kept a blog when I first arrived, quite a popular one in the U.S., and to some that meant . . . I was never exactly sure what that meant, but to some in the church it was strange, different, and alien. No pastor they knew kept a blog. No pastor in their experience had even made use of social media. I was outside of their notion or expectation of what a pastor should be.

I had a three-year contract, and to some that meant I was going to collect all of my money and go home when the contract expired. Never mind that employment contracts are standard practice in this country, especially for foreign workers, and never mind that they had not offered me more than three years. I would be here briefly, they thought, and soon I would be gone. Like all the Americans before me. On and on it went.

My first year as a stranger in this new culture was difficult. My otherness was always pronounced—in the way I spoke and dressed, and occasionally in the way I viewed the church and thought about my faith. I kept thinking, "I'm just a nice, normal Midwesterner, totally sincere in my Christian beliefs, reserved in my feelings, and mostly conservative, except on certain issues, like equal opportunities (and pay) for women. So, what is it about me that you don't like? Why can't you see me as I am?"

I could sense that some members of my new church family viewed me with deep suspicion. My probation period seemed to stretch on endlessly. A few thought the search committee had lost its collective mind: "This person calls himself a pastor?" As I mentioned, a few even left the church before my arrival.

I was guilty too

Looking back, I see that I was hardly the innocent victim. True, the stereotyping stung—and still does—but I realize now that I gave as well as I got. More than once, without a second thought, I insulted my host country.

Moving to Switzerland was initially good for my blog. Readership soared during my first months, as I expanded my themes to include observations about life in Switzerland. In my first months here, I had over 6,500 unique visitors per month. People in the U.S. regularly told me how much they enjoyed the witty observations I was making about my new culture, and I'm sure they did, almost as much I enjoyed making them.

My new Swiss friends, on the other hand, mostly kept quiet about my blog. American friends left lots of appreciative comments, while my new Swiss friends almost never commented. And now I think I understand why. I had engaged in the usual cultural stereotyping, and it was fun—until it wasn't.

A couple of examples make my point.

The Swiss are, as a people, a punctual sort. (Is a statement like that a cultural stereotype even if it is based in fact? Probably.) Their transportation system is one of the best in the world, and that's true in no small part because it's extraordinarily reliable. Trains, trams, buses, ferries, you-name-it—they all run on time. And when a train, for example, is unexpectedly late, by which I mean at most three or four minutes, you can see looks of consternation on faces at the train station. People glance at their watches and look around nervously.

And so, in one of my early blog posts, I explained the term *überpünktlich*. The Swiss, I wrote, are *überpünktlich*—in other words, almost obsessive about being on time. Five minutes early is on time, on time is late, and late is unforgivable. I also noted that in German the English question "What time is it?" is actually rendered "How late is it?" How funny. I thought that was all innocent, harmless fun. And—hey!— it was great for my blog numbers, so I kept going.

Early on I also wrote about opening my Swiss bank account. I went into great detail about how it wasn't anything like it's portrayed in books and movies. When I opened my account, no one treated me like Jason Bourne in a Robert Ludlum thriller. No one ushered me to a comfortable chair and asked me if I perhaps might like an espresso. In fact, I wrote that the whole experience was more like going to the post office because, well, it *was* the post office. The post office in Switzerland is also a bank.

As I was writing my clever, witty blog post, however, Swiss banking was undergoing a massive change. A way of life that had been carefully cultivated over several *centuries* was coming to a rather abrupt and bruising end. Banking secrecy, long a treasured feature of Swiss banking, was quickly becoming a thing of the past. And this change was affecting several members of my new church in substantial ways.

What I thought was fun turned out to be extraordinarily painful for many people. Even though they had done nothing illegal, their livelihoods and careers were jeopardized, and they were paying a steep price. Even though they never said anything, I realized that I had crossed a line. I'm afraid that I was in it mainly for the laughs.

I wish these were the only examples I could give. The truth is, I was not a sensitive, patient, or even appreciative observer of this culture. I came to Switzerland with my American sense of humor (slightly superior) and played the situation for laughs "back home." I am not proud of it.

Where the term came from

It was Walter Lippmann, in his book *Public Opinion*, who apparently first used the term "stereotype" as a metaphor for a mental picture people form based on their own cultural ideas, biases, and prejudices. So, for example, Americans are innovative, Chinese are diligent, Swiss are punctual, and Italians are expressive. And Lippmann pointed out that when we Americans meet someone from China, Switzerland, or Italy, we tend to see our cultural perception first and—this is a key point—the person second.

Lippmann was mostly positive about such stereotyping. He thought the process was necessary, useful, and even efficient. Stereotypes, he argued, make life more manageable: "For the most part we do not first see, and then define, we define first and then see. In the great blooming, buzzing confusion of the outer world we pick out what our culture has already defined for us, and we tend to perceive that which we have picked out in the form stereotyped for us by our culture."

It's an interesting argument, when you think about it, that it's too difficult, too much work, to find the person behind the stereotype. Maybe Lippmann is right that we occasionally need shortcuts to make complex systems understandable. But what happens when the stereotypes become, as they often do, quite negative, when they become disparaging, when they diminish a group of people? Stereotypes often become quite difficult to overcome.

In addition to being innovative, a widely held and very positive notion about Americans, we are often also considered to be obese, lazy, and ignorant. (I don't know for sure, but I suspect that Homer Simpson from the long-running TV series *The Simpsons* has done the stereotype of the American male no favors.) Mexicans are lazy, and millions of them are coming to the U.S. illegally. Arabs and Muslims are terrorists. The English have bad teeth. The Italians and the French are the world's best lovers. The Irish are drunks. The Swiss are *überpünktlich*. Asians are good at math. And on and on. (Notice how I have lumped several billion of the world's population under the label "Asian," while being careful to distinguish between several European countries with far smaller populations. Still another form of stereotyping.)

Positive or negative, these stereotypes have a way of obscuring the person being stereotyped.

It's not just me—it's all Americans

A favorite joke, one that never fails to get a laugh where I live, goes like this: "Why do Americans start wars? To learn geography." To much of the world, Americans are ignorant and lazy—and not just about geography. And that ignorance about the world, combined with our arrogance (and strong military), can make for a not-very-sympathetic stereotype.

One column in the local tabloid newspaper, distributed for free every evening at the train station, is titled "Neues aus Absurdistan" ("News from Absurdistan"). I started to read it on the way home from church in the evening to practice my German, but now I read it as much for what it tells me about how others view my culture.

Many of the columns (not all) are about life in the U.S. One week, for example, I read about "measles parties" in California where parents were intentionally exposing their children to measles as a way of inoculating them. One mother explained to the reporter that this was "the way God intended" children to acquire immunity to disease. In the U.S.—this was the stereotype, which I have to say was painful—God apparently takes a dim view of needles and vaccinations and is not totally in favor of the medical advances of the last century.

But not all of the stereotypes about Americans are negative. Americans can be and often are, for example, quite generous. Generally, there is no tipping in Switzerland, but Americans will tip anyway. They can't help themselves.

And Americans are generous in other ways. The budget at the church is supported in substantial ways by Americans who have highly developed habits of charitable giving. There are no tax deductions for charitable giving in Switzerland, but Americans support the church because they are in the habit of doing so.

Americans communicate warmth and spontaneity too in a way that some Swiss admire and perhaps are a bit jealous of. A couple of Swiss women came out of the door of the church one Sunday morning, and after shaking my hand they said, "We love America!" An American who has been in the country a long time overheard the comment and explained to me later what they actually meant. They may love America, which is how I heard their comment, but what they were trying to say, according to my friend, is that they loved my humor and warmth in the pulpit. Most Swiss preachers use an academic and somewhat charmless style when preaching, so my own style—stereotypically American—was to at least two Swiss women a welcome contrast.

Many of my church members have traveled to the U.S., and those who haven't look forward to doing so. The U.S. is often viewed with a mixture of fascination and revulsion. An American friend will tell me about "all the good" the U.S. is doing in the world, referring to military interventions here and there, but my new Swiss friends will express the desire that the U.S. refrain from doing so much "good."

Some of my friends from the U.S. are in the process of "relinquish-ing" (not "renouncing"—there's a difference) their U.S. citizenship, and they are doing this for tax reasons. The U.S. is apparently one of just two countries on the planet to tax their citizens for income earned abroad. So, even U.S. citizens who live abroad often have a decidedly mixed view of their country of origin, their "passport country," as some have been heard to call it.

For a country as economically and militarily powerful as the U.S., it should not be surprising that the U.S. would evoke such strong feelings and, of course, cultural stereotyping.

And I should not neglect to mention how pervasive American movies and television programming is in Europe (and undoubtedly in the rest of the world). Think of all the sitcoms and detective dramas and so forth that have been produced in the U.S. over the last 20 to 30 years, and you can imagine how our country is viewed. Not always a realistic portrait, perhaps, but realistic enough for the rest of the world to draw all sorts of conclusions.

Some harmless fun

Americans may be on the receiving end of unfortunate stereotypes, but sadly, they are guilty of a great deal of negative stereotyping among themselves.

A few years ago, at a church planting conference, a couple of attempts at humor by conference organizers, including evangelical megachurch pastor Rick Warren, went seriously awry because they played to Asian American stereotypes. Warren and conference organizers quickly issued an apology, but the response among Asian Americans was so strong that it illustrates how much of a problem cultural stereotyping remains in the U.S. and how much of an obstacle it is to the creation of a multicultural church.

In response to what happened, 80 Asian American church leaders released a letter which, among other things, stated that Asian stereotyping among American evangelicals is common and "it has to stop." Approximately 700 individuals then signed the open letter, underscoring how the incident—intended as harmless fun—actually felt to those being stereotyped.

"We are weary, hurt, and disillusioned," the letter stated, "by the continuing offensive actions." Among evangelical Christians, Asian Americans "continue to be misunderstood, misrepresented, and misjudged."

The tone of the letter suggests that the feelings behind it had been building for some time. How could something like this have gone on for so long? How could Christians, especially those in leadership positions, have been so clueless?

Cultural stereotyping persists, I suppose, because, as Lippmann argued, it appears to be helpful. We create stereotypes about others because the categories help us to understand and then predict the behavior of those people. Shouldn't we use this human tendency to our advantage?

In another chapter I argue the importance of having multicultural leadership in a multicultural church. But getting to a multicultural leadership can be difficult because, as one of my leaders put it during the first year of my ministry, "the Africans never nominate themselves." To make sure that there are Africans in leadership positions seems to require extra effort because, based on our experience, Africans tend not to nominate themselves or "to put themselves forward." Americans won't hesitate to nominate other Americans, but Africans seldom nominate other Africans.

Is it even true? Has anyone actually looked into it?

I don't know that anyone has ever conducted a study to find out if it's true, or if it's true, why it's true, but the cultural stereotype seems to have some basis in experience, some kernel of truth. And so, the church makes an extra effort to make sure there are always Africans in leadership positions. Sounds like a good thing, right? How could this kind of cultural stereotyping be unhelpful?

I have come to see that cultural stereotyping is seldom, if ever, a good thing, even when the outcome—such as having Africans in leadership positions—seems to be so good. Let me put this as bluntly and succinctly as I can: Churches that want to be multicultural need to avoid cultural stereotyping. Generalizations about other cultures always need to be examined and studied.

The first time I heard the stereotype about Africans, I was surprised. The person who spoke the words didn't seem prejudiced or bigoted. He works in a multicultural setting, after all, and prejudice or bigotry would never be tolerated there. He seemed to me to be genuinely concerned about the church and deeply committed to diversity within the leadership. In fact, he was a respected leader within the church.

I was puzzled by his remark. Africa, after all, is a big continent. Were we talking only about Kenyans? Or all of the countries of east Africa? The church members I know who are from Kenya don't seem all that shy and reserved, or reluctant to "put themselves forward." One of them is from the Masai tribe, a warrior. Are we talking about her? I doubt it. She didn't achieve all that she has professionally by failing to "put herself forward." Then who exactly are we talking about?

I don't know for sure, but here's my guess: the nominating committee had been hoping to see one name in particular in response to the annual request for nominations. And year after year that name did not appear. So, finally, someone on the nominating committee put the name on the list, perhaps with a comment about how Africans never "put themselves forward."

What concerns me more than stereotyping the population of an entire continent, however, is how we sometimes neglect to notice or understand the person behind the generalization or stereotype. I think there's a great deal at stake here. I think the issue gets to the heart of what we believe about human beings created in the image and likeness of God.

What often seems like a neutral, harmless, perhaps even helpful attempt at categorization almost inevitably has unfortunate results. Maybe not right away, but the habit can be hard to break. You know how those Africans can be.

A variation on the Golden Rule

Doesn't it make sense to treat others as you would like to be treated?

Before my move to Switzerland, I might have agreed with this simple argument. It sounds right, and of course it's biblical. But does it tell us enough about how to respond to cultural diversity within congregations? I now believe the answer to that question is no.

Let me ask you something I had not thought to ask myself before serving a multicultural congregation. What does respect look like? I want to be treated with respect, of course, and I imagine that everyone else does as well, but I now see that respect has different meanings, sometimes vastly different meanings, in different cultures. Having respect for someone might mean saying hello in the morning, or it might mean leaving that someone alone, depending on the culture. Having respect might mean making eye contact, or it might mean refraining from eye contact, once again depending on the culture. Having respect might mean being direct and blunt whenever a question is asked, or it might mean an over-abundance of politeness. Again, it depends on the culture.

One variation on the Golden Rule is sometimes referred to as the Platinum Rule: "Treat others as *they* want to be treated." In a multicultural situation, I think this is the rule we need to embrace.

It is difficult and sometimes painstaking work, however, to figure out how others want to be treated. And knowing exactly how another human being would like to be treated in every situation might well be impossible (as any married person will acknowledge). But making the effort to understand how another wants to be treated will at least change the frame of reference from "how I want to be treated is probably how all other people want to be treated" or "how a person from one culture wants to be treated is more than likely how a person from another culture wants to be treated."

I had no idea until recently that major corporations and larger businesses have begun to devote a great deal of time to this issue—often under the not-very-pastoral-sounding term "diversity management." The idea, greatly oversimplified, is that a leader needs to understand the people she is leading in order to have the most effective work relationships.

Here are some questions that business leaders in multicultural settings are having to ask themselves, and these questions are useful for pastors and church leaders in multicultural churches as well:

- Do you test your assumptions before acting on them?
- Do you believe that there is only one right way of doing things, or that there might be a number of valid ways to accomplish the same goal?
- Do you have honest relationships with each staff member you supervise? Are you comfortable with each of them? Do you know what motivates them, what their goals are, how they like to be recognized?
- Are you able to give negative feedback to someone who is culturally different from you?
- Do you rigorously examine your team's (or church's) existing policies, practices, and procedures to ensure that they do not differentially impact different groups? When they do, do you change them?
- Do you take immediate action with people you supervise when they behave in ways that show disrespect for others in the workplace, such as inappropriate jokes and offensive terms?

It occurred to me when I came across this list that expectations in the church should be at least as rigorous as they are in the workplace.

One of my colleagues in an English-speaking congregation not far from Zürich told me that when he was called to be pastor, the expectations for him went beyond language learning to this other field of diversity management. Before he unpacked a single box of books, he found himself attending a class about cultural assumptions (and stereotyping). I think back to the churches I have served over the years and wonder how much easier my transitions would have been if I had had a similar class or seminar.

Jesus and the Syrophoenician woman

One of the most perplexing encounters in the Gospels is a cross-cultural conversation between Jesus and a Syrophoenician woman (Mark 7:24–30, also recorded in Matthew 15:21–28). Jesus speaks with people from other cultures elsewhere in the Gospels (his encounter with the Samaritan woman in John 4 comes to mind), but in this case the person's otherness is obviously emphasized and in some ways is more important to the story than the healing which happens at the end. The person who is introduced to us is a woman, a Gentile, and a Syrophoenician, three good reasons why a first-century Jewish man might not want to speak with her.

What Jesus is doing so far from home—in this story, interestingly, *he* is the foreigner—is one mysterious element in the story. What is even more mysterious is how he responds to a woman who asks—and is extraordinarily *persistent* about asking—Jesus to heal her daughter.

At first Jesus seems rude to the woman. He ignores her and seems to refuse to help, which would have been uncharacteristic of him. It is only after the woman responds—in quite a clever way—that Jesus heals: "For saying that, you may go—the demon has left your daughter." He seems genuinely taken with her intelligence and wit. It seems to have been her artful response, in fact, that cut through layers of cultural stereotyping.

Commentators have offered all sorts of explanations for what Jesus says to this woman, but the fact remains that he used the word "dog" to describe her. Jews often referred to Gentiles in this way, and apparently—for historical reasons—Syrophoenicians were particularly disliked by Jews. If anyone deserved to be called a "dog," in the mind of a first-century Jew, it was a Syrophoenician.

Jesus, it is sometimes noted, uses the diminutive form of the word here—"little dog" or perhaps "puppy"—but even at that, the word is disturbing, isn't it?

It is also sometimes noted that Jesus speaks the word in an interesting way—as part of a riddle—but, again, the word is still there. The first and most obvious cultural stereotype about this woman is that she is a "dog," and there is no getting around it: it's an ugly word, a slur, not something we would ever expect to hear from the lips of Jesus.

I have always liked New Testament scholar F. F. Bruce's suggestion that there must have been "a twinkle in his eye as he spoke." In other words, Jesus spoke the word in this situation with a knowing look. According to this view, Jesus uses the word intentionally and playfully to get a response. The woman knew what he meant, and it wasn't derogatory, not the way he said it. He was treating her the way she wanted to be treated.

Whatever really happened between Jesus and this woman, Jesus was well aware that he was speaking to someone of a different cultural and religious background. Whoever witnessed the encounter was aware of this as well and thought the encounter was important enough to remember.

Here's what I have always liked about this story: Jesus looked beyond the obvious cultural and religious differences and acted, as he always did, with compassion. Where others would have seen a cultural stereotype, Jesus clearly saw a human being, someone in need. And it was to that human being that he reached out in compassion and love.

CHAPTER EIGHT

Consider What the Flag Might Mean

I may not be the right person to write this chapter.

I was seventeen when the Vietnam War was nearing its end, but the ending to that war was a protracted one. As peace negotiations dragged on, an unprecedented bombing campaign continued, and young men like me were still being drafted into military service.

My theological training at seventeen was limited, though not entirely missing. It consisted of twice-weekly worship services throughout my childhood, plus Sunday school and midweek catechism classes. Somehow I got the idea into my head that war was wrong. I thought I saw a contradiction between what I was learning at church and what was happening half a world away.

I tried talking to my pastor about it, but didn't get very far. He told me that he would not accompany me to a meeting with my draft board where I hoped to make my case. That turned out to be a serious setback because conscientious objection was allowed then only on the basis of a *religious* objection to war. I thought I could make a reasonably strong religious objection to war, but it turns out that I was naive. My pastor reminded me that I had not grown up in a historic peace church. I was not, for example, a Mennonite, and my own church was agnostic about the war in Vietnam. It would be hard to prove my case.

In order to avoid walking into the meeting with the draft board by myself, I asked my father to go with me. As a World War II veteran who had volunteered for the privilege of serving his country at a time of war, he might have been an unlikely choice to act as my representative. But he came with me. He also wrote a fine letter of support for my file, a letter I still treasure. Unfortunately, a parent's endorsement doesn't count for much in these matters. It was really only the religious angle the draft board cared about.

I remember sitting across a table from a group of men I did not know, explaining to them how important my faith was to me, how it affected every part of my life, and (importantly) how my faith gave me serious reservations about this particular war. They did not seem impressed by my presentation.

I also remember my pre-induction physical. I boarded a bus in Grand Rapids, and along with 60 to 70 other young men I traveled to Detroit, where I spent a day in my underwear enduring a thorough physical examination. This was the only test in my life that I was certain to pass just because I showed up to take it. My eyes, ears, nose, heart, joints, etc. were all deemed healthy enough for me to be trained for combat.

All I needed, as soon as I turned eighteen, was a letter in the mail directing me to report for basic training.

As it turned out, no such letter came. The war finally came to an end, and I have spent the better part of my life trying to make sense of that early experience. For an entire generation of men—those who went and those who didn't—that war was a defining experience—not in the way a previous war had been a defining experience for my father and his generation, but in a different, sometimes more troubling way.

I know this much: I came of age at a time when my country's flaws and shortcomings were on full display. Trust in authority had—for good reason—been seriously eroded. It's true that I had the right and freedom to challenge what I considered to be wrong, for which I will always be grateful, but at a formative time in my life I learned a basic lesson in ultimate allegiances: faith in God and love for country are not always compatible.

I am as proud as anyone to be an American. I am usually first on my feet, with my hand over my heart, to sing the National Anthem at sporting events. I cheer U.S. athletes in Olympic competition, and I always expect the U.S. to win many more medals than any other country. On the morning of September 11, 2001, no one felt more American than I did.

So, it's interesting that at this point in my life I should find myself living outside the U.S. in what is a decidedly multinational setting, a church setting where love of country is seldom, if ever, discussed, where there is almost a reluctance to say much about national pride. Outside the World Cup for men's soccer (*Fußball-Weltmeisterschaft der Männer*), which comes around only every four years, no one says all that much about their country, at least not the way I am used to hearing it expressed.

What role does patriotism or national pride play in a church where many nationalities are represented? Is it okay to be proud of one's country in a setting like that? And if so, what would that look like? What sort of patriotic behavior contributes to the health and vitality of a church (and what sort of behavior does not)? I may be the only person at my church who thinks about such questions.

Displaying the flag

For most of my ministry, the relationship between faith and patriotism has played itself out around the unlikely question, "Is it okay to display a U.S. flag in the church sanctuary?" I'm guessing you have an opinion about that. Everyone seems to, and I think I have heard just about all of them.

I served a church early in my ministry that displayed a flag in the sanctuary. I had never seen a flag in church before—it was startling to me—and being a young and inexperienced pastor, I decided without consulting anyone to move it to another location in the church—not into a closet, but far away from the worship space.

Interestingly, I found that the flag had been moved back into the sanctuary for the following Sunday. The person who brought it back from its brief banishment told me that he agreed with me about how shabby the old flag looked (he assumed that was the reason I moved it) and that he was going to buy new flags—a U.S. flag *and* a Christian flag!—with shiny brass hardware, so that we could all be proud of them.

I didn't know what a Christian flag was, but he seemed to know a lot about flags and flag etiquette and explained to me how the U.S. flag should always be displayed in "a place of honor," which seemed to be right behind the pulpit and plainly visible over my right shoulder.

I do not remember that any of this was covered in my seminary classes about worship, so I had to rely on my pastoral instincts to handle the situation. I told him that we would bring in the flags for special occasions, like national holidays, and he seemed pleased with the compromise. Or maybe he realized that I was not going to back down. Either way, he bought us brand-new flags with shiny brass hardware.

The next church I served had no flags in the sanctuary, or anywhere else on church property, and when someone offered to donate a flag pole to the church so that the U.S. flag could be displayed outdoors, visible from the street, the church board rather quickly turned down the gift, as if to say, "What part of 'no flags on church property' don't you understand?"

I was surprised by the different set of expectations and norms that this other church had, and what I learned was that Americans are clearly not of one mind about how faith and country, church and state, should get along.

In my travels around the world, I don't recall seeing many national flags displayed in church sanctuaries. One time, during a summer mission trip to Peru, a pastor in a tiny village in the central highlands of that country somehow managed to find a U.S. flag, which he draped over the pulpit in honor of our presence in the church. I was moved by his thoughtfulness and posed with him behind the pulpit for a photograph. But for him this was nothing more than an act of hospitality. After we left, I am pretty sure he put away the flag, until the next mission team came along.

For many U.S. church members, the flag is, without a doubt, a matter of patriotism, and many would say that it should be displayed out of gratitude for the religious freedom Americans enjoy. I understand that reasoning, and I feel the same gratitude, but mostly because of my personal history, whenever I see a U.S. flag in a church, I find myself thinking, "Who or what are we worshiping here?"

When early Christians declared that "Jesus is Lord" (1 Cor. 12:3), they were also implicitly saying that "Caesar is not." The early church's first affirmation of faith had decidedly political overtones, and the ultimate allegiance of those early Christians was not in doubt. They said the words fearlessly and sometimes paid a price for doing so. The relationship between church and state at the time was never a cozy one.

The apostle Paul was quite clear about being "subject to the governing authorities" (Rom. 13:1) and praying "for kings and all who are in authority" (1 Tim. 2:2), and Jesus cleverly answered a question meant to trick him by saying, "Render therefore unto Caesar the things that are Caesar's and unto God the things that are God's" (Matt. 22:21). The Bible has a great deal to say about the relationship between one's faith and temporal authority, but nowhere is there a suggestion that the two always fit comfortably together.

On the contrary, people of faith down through the centuries have often been called on to declare their ultimate allegiance.

A special relationship

American Christians, I've decided, have what can only be considered a unique perspective about God and country. According to a recent study by LifeWay Research, 53 percent of all Americans believe that "God has a special relationship" with the United States. Among those who identify as evangelicals, 45 years and older, that figure is a staggering 71 percent.

My guess is that if the Swiss were asked whether or not God had a special relationship with Switzerland, they would be confused by the question. Though church attendance is not high in Switzerland—or anywhere else in Europe—a certain kind of religiosity runs deep in Swiss culture. There is a cross, of course, on the national flag, which is remarkable when you think about it, but there is more.

At the center of every village is a very well-maintained church, often though not always Protestant. Every church has a bell tower, and the bells ring every fifteen minutes, day or night, and much more on holidays and Sunday mornings and sometimes for no apparent reason. I found the bells charming when I first moved here, and then less charming as the months went by.

But the Swiss love their church bells and hear in them a reminder of their identity. The Swiss seem to understand that the church is an integral part of their culture, and so, even though they do not attend Sunday morning worship with the same frequency that Americans do, they are very reluctant to let go of the church's symbolic presence at the center of their lives.

Maybe more Swiss than I imagine would say that "God has a special relationship" with Switzerland.

Patriotism and multicultural churches

There is no national flag on display in the French Reformed Church where the International Protestant Church of Zürich meets for worship each Sunday morning, and there is no national flag in the Evangelical-Methodist Church where we meet each Sunday evening. That the French Church is owned by the state church, or *Landeskirche*, and is therefore closely linked to the government, makes no difference. There is no Swiss flag, nor would anyone expect to find one there.

I suppose that, if we really wanted to, we could move one in after the other congregation departs. After all, we rearrange the sanctuary slightly before our own service begins. But no one to my knowledge, certainly not the Swiss, has ever suggested that we display a flag.

And then there's the question: Which flag would we display?

The Swiss are proud of their flag and fly it everywhere except, as I mentioned, in worship spaces. The distinctive white cross on a red background—and the square shape—make for a bright and unique design. (The Vatican is the only other sovereign state with a square flag.) Look around any village in the country, and you will see the flag everywhere and attached to nearly everything. The Swiss are not overly sentimental about most things, but there is an undeniable attachment to the flag and the history it represents. Switzerland's refusal to join the European Union (as well as its refusal to join the monetary union known as the Euro) is a strong indication of the Swiss people's fiercely independent feelings. They almost always prefer to go their own way.

If any country—other than the U.S., of course—were to display a flag in a worship space, you would think that it would be Switzerland.

Interestingly, most of my church members are utterly unaware of the flag-in-worship controversy in the U.S. Even during a recent African festival, when our worship featured African music and dancing and clothing, no one asked if perhaps the flag of Kenya or South Africa or Ethiopia could be displayed. In hindsight, maybe we should have done it, maybe it would have added something to the occasion, but it seems telling to me that no one even thought to suggest it. Americans may well be unique in their desire to bring a national flag into a worship space.

What I have learned is that for much of the world the presence of a flag in worship would seem odd and out of place. We gather to worship God, members of my church would say, not a symbol of national pride.

Fourth of July at First Baptist Church

In the community where I served before moving to Zürich, the large downtown Baptist church always had a well-publicized patriotic celebration in worship on the Sunday closest to the Fourth of July.

It was something people talked about and looked forward to. Members of my Presbyterian church sometimes became Baptists for a day in order to attend this service. "It's something you can enjoy over and over again," they would tell me. On this particular July morning the Baptist service had the look and feel of a Broadway show, including a full orchestra, indoor fireworks display, impressive military color guard, and an enormous American flag which came sweeping down out of the ceiling at the end of the service. On this one Sunday each year, the Baptist church was "standing room only" for all of its morning services.

Here's what I found so startling: Everyone I knew treated it as entirely normal and kind of exciting. A Christmas pageant in December (with impressive-looking camels for the wise men) and a patriotic Fourth of July celebration a few months later—what a wonderful church! And look at the crowds! (Lost to them, apparently, is the historical irony that the patron saint of Baptists in America, Roger Williams, a founder of the first and oldest Baptist congregation, the First Baptist Church of Providence, Rhode Island, was the greatest proponent of the separation of church and state and was most responsible for installing that principle in the First Amendment to the Constitution.)

I work on Sundays, as I have mentioned, so during my years in Florida I never personally witnessed this patriotic celebration at First Baptist Church, but that didn't stop me from forming an opinion about it. My opinion was that I didn't like it. Frankly, it seemed wrong to me on so many levels, but mostly I kept that opinion to myself. So many others, after all, loved it and were deeply moved by it. They liked it so much that they wondered why we Presbyterians didn't—at the very least—sing "America the Beautiful" in our church on that Sunday.

Now that I have some distance to reflect—nearly 5,000 miles, as a matter of fact—I find myself thinking back to those Fourth of July services at First Baptist Church. You might be surprised to learn this, but that Baptist church has one of the most culturally diverse congregations in all of South Florida—far more diverse than my own church at the time. They took pride in their racial and ethnic diversity and made this fact a part of their marketing plan.

And yes, I was jealous about that. Somehow they had found a way to do something that very few other American churches seem able to do. They had a growing multicultural congregation.

But it doesn't make sense, does it? What does an over-the-top patriotic display around the Fourth of July mean to all of those people from other cultures?

For some people the service is undoubtedly a crash course in American-style patriotic fervor—in other words, not offensive, but enlightening. You find pretty much the same thing every weekend at a college football game or at a NASCAR race. The military color guards, the fighter-jet flyovers, the enormous American flags—they are not-so-subtle reminders about what matters in American life.

For other people the service must be a welcome thing, especially if coming to the U.S. meant escaping a painful and oppressive situation back home. Cuban immigrants to the U.S.—the ones I have met—are some of the most fervent American patriots you will ever find. I am guessing that they too have no complaints about the annual Fourth of July service.

But I am concerned about the rest, those who might feel confused or left out.

Writing recently on the Gospel Coalition blog, Trevin Wax told the story of doing mission work a few years ago in Romania. After learning the language and settling into ministry in a village church, he remembers asking the pastor why the church didn't do a special service in December celebrating Unification Day (Romania's national holiday) and why the national flag wasn't displayed in the sanctuary.

The pastor gave him an odd look and said, "The only way we'd bring a Romanian flag into our sanctuary is if we brought in flags from all over the world."

"To show you do missions?" he asked.

"No, to show we are the church," the pastor said.

A few years later, Wax reports that he attended a Sunday morning worship service back in the U.S. and that the congregation was singing patriotic songs. At one point the congregation was even asked to pledge allegiance to the U.S. flag. He noticed that his wife, who was a Romanian citizen, was not participating. A young woman from another country who had recently come to faith and had been newly baptized was also not singing and not pledging allegiance.

They both stood quietly, not participating, not really sure what to make of worship that day.

Wax says that "the oddness of the scene struck me. We were in a worship service with fellow believers, including one just baptized, who could not participate. Something made me feel uneasy, but it took me a while to realize why."

Incorporating national symbols and patriotic pride into worship has always seemed problematic to me, but since moving to Switzerland I have begun to see even more clearly the difficulty and awkwardness that occur when Christian faith tries to align itself too closely with one country.

An American Thanksgiving

One time, at the church I served in Wheaton, Illinois, I invited a fine young pastor from Brazil, who was doing graduate work at Wheaton College, to preach the sermon at our Thanksgiving Eve worship service. Only later did it occur to me that this was a poor choice. My dear friend from Brazil had never experienced an American Thanksgiving. What could he possibly say on Thanksgiving Eve that would have meaning for us?

A great deal, as it turns out. He organized his sermon in the form of a letter to his mother back in Brazil, explaining to her the meaning of the holiday and why Americans are so attached to it. He admitted to his mother (and to us) that he was moved by the holiday and what it represented. In the end, it was a wonderful Thanksgiving sermon, quite possibly the best one I have ever heard. But for my friend it required a delicate balancing of loyalties. He was of course grateful to the U.S. for the opportunity to study here, but he was also proud of his own Brazilian heritage. Somehow—this is an important, though rare, skill in a preacher—he was able to bring all of those threads together in one sermon.

On a recent Thanksgiving, our first in Switzerland, I was invited to the home of American friends, where my wife and I were treated to a meal with turkey, stuffing, cranberry sauce, mashed potatoes, green bean casserole, pumpkin pie, and a few other staples of the traditional feast. The goal of the menu was familiarity, not originality.

Most of us around the table were Americans. A few were Asians by way of America. A few had come to Switzerland and were in the process of relinquishing their U.S. passports for tax reasons. And a few others—I was in this latter group—had no idea how long we would be in the country.

Before the prayer of thanksgiving for God's goodness and protection, which is another tradition that seems to go along with the meal, we took turns expressing our own individual reasons for being thankful. We gave thanks for jobs, enough to eat, family and friends, and our church (the pastor was present, after all).

I'm glad we did it. Had a Thanksgiving dinner, that is. Thanksgiving feels odd when you're so far from home. It can be a lonely day. No one else in the country is celebrating, except for the expats. It is a work day for most, like any other. The trains and trams and buses are as crowded as any other day.

But for Americans there is a powerful tug of memory. There is an awareness that across the ocean people we know, our families and friends, are coming together and enjoying a holiday that emphasizes close ties and country and gratitude.

Of all the holidays I miss each year, I miss Thanksgiving the most.

And that's interesting because Thanksgiving, along with the Fourth of July, is probably the most American of holidays. A few other countries have a Thanksgiving Day, including Switzerland, but Thanksgiving Day in the U.S. is a day when a national story is remembered, when gratitude is expressed, when God's name is spoken, when faith (however fleeting) seems genuine and important. (The Swiss version of Thanksgiving is known as the Federal Day of Thanksgiving, Repentance, and Prayer—*Eidgenössischer Dank-, Buss- und Bettag*—and occurs on the third Sunday of September. It hardly compares to the American version of the day and seems to slip by without much notice.)

It is in our observance of Thanksgiving, it seems to me, that Americans are most successful in their attempt to blend faith and love for country.

Dare to be a Daniel

A formative song from my childhood—I learned it in my kindergarten Sunday school class—was "Dare to Be a Daniel."

The story of Daniel in the lions' den (Daniel 6) is one of the most well known and perhaps beloved in all of Scripture. According to the story, Daniel was among a group of Israelites "of the royal family and of the nobility, young men without physical defect and handsome, versed in every branch of wisdom, endowed with knowledge and insight, and competent to serve in the king's palace" (1:3–4).

As I reread those words now, I am struck all over again by how engaging the story was to a young reader. I had no trouble identifying with Daniel or his friends. I wasn't from a royal family, of course, but good children's stories stimulate the imagination. Of course I could have been Daniel.

In the story—after a bit of dream interpretation and a scary incident involving a fiery furnace and Daniel's three friends—an edict was issued forbidding people to worship anyone or anything for 30 days. It was a trap, of course, set by Daniel's enemies, and it worked, because Daniel "continued to go to his house, which had windows in its upper room open toward Jerusalem, and to get down on his knees three times a day to pray to his God and praise him, just as he had done previously" (6:10).

No edict would prevent a young man like Daniel from worshiping his God!

Daniel had been set up because his enemies in the story knew that he would never betray his God. King Darius liked Daniel—because he was smart and good-looking—but, reluctantly, he had to send Daniel to the lions' den, where Daniel was to die a particularly gruesome death. Except, as we all know, he didn't.

"My God sent his angel and shut the lions' mouths so that they would not hurt me," Daniel explained to the king (6:22), who was enormously relieved that Daniel had survived the night. Somewhat annoyed with Daniel's enemies, however, the king threw them, "their children, and their wives" (6:24) into the lions' den instead. "Before they reached the bottom of the den," the story tells us, "the lions overpowered them and broke all their bones into pieces."

No one in my class thought to wonder about that rather harsh detail at the end of the story. (What did the children or wives do, after all, to deserve that punishment?) We were too busy absorbing the challenging truth of the story—namely, that a young Israelite man who placed allegiance to God above his allegiance to the king was rewarded for that faithfulness. In other words, it was possible to defy an unjust civil authority, obey God, and live. That's what biblical heroes did.

I'm not sure what the Sunday school curriculum intended for us to learn, but what I learned and internalized was something very simple: be ready to give your life, if necessary, in service to a higher truth, a just cause, like worshiping the God of Israel and not the king of Persia.

Now that I think about it, my Sunday school classmates and I were martyrs in training. From that Sunday morning when I first learned this story, I was waiting for my opportunity to take a stand. And then, of course, the song reinforced everything we heard:

Dare to be a Daniel,
Dare to stand alone!
Dare to have a purpose firm!
Dare to make it known.

Daniel and the other Old Testament prophets had complicated relationships with the state. Contemporary readers of these books of the Bible seem to miss this dimension. Most people I know, members of the churches I serve, are looking for clues and hints about the future, especially the birth of a messiah. And though those clues and hints are there, the prophets themselves devoted their lives to the thankless work of speaking out against injustice and idolatry. The job description of a prophet was, in large part, to speak out against kings and their advisors when they acted unfaithfully, when they lost sight of God.

Few prophets had an easy time of it, but Jeremiah had a harder time than most. He hated his calling and at one point called his life "a fountain of tears" (Jer. 9:1). His words were so difficult to hear that the king tried to have him killed.

You could argue, I suppose, that the prophets thought of themselves as the loyal opposition. They spoke as they did because they loved their country, not because they hated it. But it is clear that they steadfastly maintained their independence, their position of being "over against" the king. There was never a doubt as to their ultimate allegiance.

When I find myself in worship, I want to know that what unites the people of God is not their patriotic fervor, but a God to whom all kings, queens, presidents, and prime ministers owe their allegiance. Oddly, I am more aware of that truth here in this multinational setting than I ever was in the U.S.

CHAPTER NINE

It's Not the Music (or the Worship Style)

The New City Church of Los Angeles recently posted this description on its website:

> We are probably one of the most diverse churches you can imagine. We are about pretty much evenly spread out ethnically; we have 18–22 percent in each major ethnic group: Latinos, Anglos, Asians, blacks, and multi-racial. We are about a third from Skid Row, a third from the lofts, and a third from outside of Downtown. Our church is beautiful in its diversity. As you get to know one another, you will start to appreciate one another's beauty and truly learn to love people who are different than yourself. This will stretch your soul and help you love more broadly and deeply. We believe that this is the call of the gospel of Jesus Christ.

What's most striking to me about that description, and there is obviously a great deal that is striking, is this sentence: "Our church is beautiful in its diversity."

The website nowhere (that I could find) uses the usual language about "contemporary" or "traditional" worship. I might have thought to include that language on my own church website. I have known many church members over the years who would want to include that language. But the New City Church does not include it—anywhere.

I suppose the photos and the text give enough hints about what to expect in the church's worship life, but New City Church doesn't start there when describing itself. Maybe, I don't know, but maybe the expectation is that a church with a name like "New City Church" will feature worship that is more contemporary than traditional, more drums and amplification equipment than robed choirs and organs.

Still, the language that is used is not about worship style, but about relationships, about learning to love people who are different from ourselves, about being stretched to "love more broadly and deeply."

I think that's significant.

The New City Church of Los Angeles has obviously discovered what I also discovered very early in my experience of serving a multicultural church—namely, that worship style is a relatively insignificant factor in the health and vitality of a multicultural church. In fact, worship style is at best a *secondary* factor in what helps a multicultural church to thrive.

I don't mean to suggest that worship style (or music) is unimportant. It certainly is to me, and it is to quite a few other people I know. We often talk about music, as a matter of fact, as though it is the *most* important feature of church life. But what I have discovered—much to my surprise—is that worship style (or music) is at best secondary to other features—mostly the quality of relationships within the church.

Even as I write these words, I expect that there will be members of my church who will want to argue the point. I know this because we have had these arguments many times, occasionally in language that we later regret. We have also attached articles to emails to bolster our point of view, though usually to little effect. Some church members will even point to a mega church across town—yes, Switzerland has them too, though not many—where the music is contemporary and the large number of worshipers is undeniable.

"See," they will say, "that's what makes a church grow."

You won't be surprised to learn that these arguments seldom get us anywhere, and so I hope it is helpful to gather some data, to take a careful look at some multicultural churches that thrive.

What a recent study shows

Gerardo Marti is a sociologist who teaches at Davidson College, a Presbyterian school in Davidson, North Carolina. He recently undertook an in-depth study of worship music in what he calls "multiethnic churches." His study sample consisted of 12 "successfully integrated" churches in the U.S.

In 2012 he published his findings in the book *Worship Across the Racial Divide: Religious Music and the Multiracial Congregation*, and those findings are receiving a great deal of attention, as they should.

His research largely confirms what I have experienced for myself—that the "success" of multicultural churches lies less in a particular style of music and more in the use of music to form lasting cross-cultural connections in the congregation.

To put this another way, it's less about the rhythm, and more about the relationships. I suspect this will be counter-intuitive for some.

I have found denominational resources, for example, that give instructions for becoming a multicultural church, and often these resources begin with instructions about how to introduce new styles of music. One major denomination in the U.S. (not my own) provides resources at its website for "How to Worship in Multicultural Churches," with instructions for introducing drums, guitar, and rhythm instruments.

I approached this material, as you might imagine, with a great deal of hope and expectation, mostly because my own experience with multicultural worship was so limited. But I was disappointed and surprised at what I found.

The resources contain the claim, for example, that "multicultural worship experiences are more successful, interesting, and meaningful when they are as musical and visual as possible. Music is indeed a universal language!"

That's quite a claim, but what was it based on? Music may indeed be a "universal language"—I'm not entirely sure what that means—but music in my experience doesn't seem to be the primary vehicle to achieve a thriving multiracial, multicultural church.

If you're looking to have a more diverse church, introducing new styles of music may not be the place to start. Interview the leaders of churches with diverse and thriving congregations, Marti writes, and they will tell you the same thing: It's not the music.

Marti argues that what "succeeds" musically in multiracial churches is not a particular type of music—or even the quality of its presentation—but rather "people of various backgrounds practicing together, spending time together, singing together, and worshiping together."

Imagine your child (or your niece or your nephew) performing a musical piece at a school recital or with a church children's choir, Marti writes. What do the adults do? No matter what sort of music is played, no matter how well or how poorly it is performed, the adults will cheer, often while standing, and usually filled with joy and pride. The point is not whether the children "did well." The point is that they are our children, and we are proud of them for what they have done.

Similarly—and this, I believe, is central to Marti's argument—worship music is defined less by a particular sound and more by the activity that encompasses it. And since worship is inherently participatory, it is in this participation that relationships are formed.

In fact, Marti goes so far as to state that not only is this true in less diverse (or monocultural) churches, but that this is especially true in multicultural churches.

One more study

Could the global church perhaps be helpful here as well? I think it can.

Three faculty members at the School of Theology, the University of Pretoria, undertook a study which was similar to Gerardo Marti's work, though in a South African context. The three researchers—Suzanne Van der Merwe, Hennie Pieterse, and Cas Wepener—studied churches in three different traditions: Dutch Reformed, Roman Catholic, and Charismatic.

In one of the churches they visited, a Dutch Reformed church, they wrote that "you will find South African (black, brown, Indian, and white) citizens, Asian (Chinese and South Korean) citizens, as well as citizens from other African countries (Congo, Kenya, Zimbabwe) attending the service. This sort of diversity—perhaps striking to churchgoers in the U.S.—seems fairly typical in the South African churches that were studied.

To a number of focus groups within these congregations, they put this question: "What . . . do congregants/pastors need when churches and worship are multicultural?" As with the Marti study, the responses given by South African Christians focused on relationships, especially the relational skills of worship leaders and pastors. Church members wanted to find in their leaders "people skills, understanding of different cultures, flexibility, sensitivity, tolerance, and a specific personality type—someone who is open and friendly towards people."

The single most frequently mentioned characteristic of a *member* of a multicultural church in South Africa was "a teachable spirit." As one focus group participant put it: "We can all teach each other something, we must be prepared to learn from each other."

The South African study went beyond the search for characteristics of a thriving multicultural church. Given the unique context, with its social and racial turmoil, the researchers wanted to know what it was in these churches that provided social cohesion and opportunities for reconciliation. Still, the results are useful and, in my experience, striking.

And here they are, the qualities present in South African congregations that somehow—in spite of tall odds—are able to come together in worship and church life:

- *An open and friendly atmosphere during the worship service*
- *Fellowship*
- *A teachable spirit*
- *Telling stories to one another*
- *Making an effort to reach out to strangers (hospitality)*
- *The power of forgiveness*
- *Unified in Jesus Christ*
- *Context*
- *Leadership*

A vintage model

What I discovered when I first arrived at the International Protestant Church of Zürich was a morning worship service that resembled Presbyterian worship in the United States in, let's say, the 1950s.

I do not mean that as a criticism.

Having grown up in the 1950s, I feel a fair amount of nostalgia for this era. I started going to church during this decade—in fact, there was no such thing as a church nursery at the time—and I became very comfortable with the dynamics and rhythms of this particular era of worship. For the first 20 years or so of my life, this worship style was all I knew. And I never thought I would see it again.

But in the early years of the twenty-first century, to walk into an English-speaking church in the middle of Switzerland's largest city, and to find a congregation that uses the same order of worship (and the same hymns!) I came to know in my childhood was, well, unexpected. And then to feel everyone's participation, to hear everyone singing those old hymns—it was . . . how do I say this?

It's a little like finding an old station wagon with wood side panels in the parking lot. In mint condition no less! You don't expect to see one of those. You expect to see newer models and sleeker profiles. But there it is, and your eyes are drawn to it. You think, with a bit of smug satisfaction, "They sure don't make them like that anymore."

So, you walk over to get a better look. It certainly is curious.

And then you notice that the people in the congregation are not old. You have to look hard, as a matter of fact, to find an older adult. They're there, of course, but there aren't many of them.

Come to think of it, I feel old here, and not because I am breaking down and getting rusty, but because the congregation is so young—young adults and young families with young children. Along one side of the balcony you see teenagers too, lots of them, and they are sitting with their friends because it's a tradition in the church that that's where they sit on Sunday morning, pretending not to pay attention, but hearing every word that's spoken. (I know because of the questions they ask after the service.)

I still don't know exactly what to make of the worship style, but believe me when I say I am in no hurry to make changes. When the church had its start more than 50 years ago, it adopted a worship style that most people knew and were comfortable with, and with a few tweaks and modifications along the way that's the worship style we have today. Over the years the church has come to be known in the city and surrounding villages for this style of worship—for other things too, of course, but certainly for this.

Honesty requires me to point out two other details.

One is that early in the church's history a relationship developed with the Zürich Opera House. Not a formal relationship, certainly, but singers and musicians, some of the finest in the world, would make their way over to the church on Sunday morning and provide the music.

Since these singers and musicians are classically trained and steeped in a particular style, the music life of the church has clearly tilted in this direction too, although these singers and musicians regularly sing and play in other styles as well.

The other detail I need to mention is that a few years ago, partly in response to the desire on the part of a few members for a different worship style, an evening worship was started. The singers and musicians at this new service have no less musical skill, but they are clearly what most people would recognize as a band or praise team. They play guitars, drums, and electronic keyboard, and they use sound amplification equipment—lots of it. And they typically play music written in the last 20 to 30 years.

Though the evening service has a loyal and passionate congregation, almost entirely different from that of the morning service, the reputation of the church, I dare say, has been built not on what happens in the evening, but on what happens in the morning.

The question I have asked myself over and over since becoming pastor is how a church can thrive with such an old-fashioned and (for many people) out-of-date, even antique, style of worship. Why do people from all over the world—every tribe, tongue, and nation—come together on Sunday morning and agree to worship the way we do?

I don't know the answer to that question. No one does. But I have a guess. And my guess is that it's not the worship style that brings us together.

It's not the music either, lovely as it usually is.

Sojourners

IPC does not own any real estate or church buildings or even office space, so the morning worship service takes place in rented space, which happens to be a French Reformed Church, owned and maintained by the *Landeskirche* or state church. My congregation enters after the French congregation departs, a transition that happens smoothly most weeks. Evening worship takes place in an Evangelical-Methodist Church building across the street from the French Church. The church offices are in still another nearby building.

The French Church is quite an old building—practically ancient by

U.S. standards—and not particularly inviting. The number of steps leading to the worship space makes the church inaccessible to all but the most able. The church has stone walls too, which create interesting acoustical challenges.

The architecture undoubtedly lends itself to a more traditional style of worship, though, to be honest, the French-speaking congregation with whom we share this space is now largely African. And their worship style, from what I hear when I stand outside waiting to get in, is far livelier than ours.

The French Church organ is in the back of the church—in the balcony—and that's where the choir sits as well.

To complete the picture, I should mention that I wear a black Geneva gown to lead worship, and I climb 14 steps to an old pulpit, where I am almost at eye level with the people sitting in the balcony. A few years ago the trend seemed clear that all pastors would eventually wear Hawaiian shirts and jeans and would pace back and forth on a stage while preaching. Instead of following that trend, I seem to have leaped backward a few centuries.

My pastoral colleague loves the setting even more than I do and has taken to wearing preaching tabs. Most Sundays Scottie Williams looks uncannily like an African-American version of the sixteenth-century Reformer Ulrich Zwingli, who once preached at a church which is only a stone's throw from where the French Church stands today.

So, traditional worship space, with pipe organ, choir loft, and elevated pulpit. Worship leaders who dress for the sixteenth century. These are not the features one would expect of a thriving multicultural church—or a thriving church of any kind. In many places in the U.S., in fact, these would be the features of an aging, declining congregation. Developers would be eying the property as a future antique shop or trendy restaurant.

And yet, our morning worship thrives. It is noisy and alive. Most Sundays all of the seats are filled, and occasionally worshipers must stand in the back because there is no place to sit. Beyond that, more than a hundred children have come forward on a regular basis for a children's message.

This is not a dying, declining church. By any measure this is a church that is alive and thriving.

A ritual I have come to love

We have a ritual on Sundays at IPC, something I look forward to each week. But first a word about that word "ritual."

Where I grew up, ritual was always a bad thing. For one thing, maybe the most important thing, ritual reeked of Roman Catholicism. Catholics had rituals. We Protestants didn't. It was that simple.

And when we spoke about ritual, the word was usually preceded by another word—"empty."

Ritual by definition, we would argue, was empty. In other words, mindlessly going through the motions.

The ritual I am referring to here, however, is neither empty nor mindless. In fact, it's a high point in worship. I have been taught over the years in evangelism seminars that I should never make visitors feel uncomfortable—for example, by asking them to stand and identify themselves or to wear a nametag identifying them as visitors.

It was best to let them be anonymous, I was told, and so mostly, over the years, I have followed that advice. Until I became the pastor of an international, multicultural church.

To be honest, it wasn't just my training. I thought I might tire of repeating this same thing week after week, but the truth is I get more and more interested each week. I look forward to doing it, and everyone else does as well. On the rare occasions when I have forgotten to do it, someone reminds me that I missed it.

Which, I suppose, is the best kind of ritual.

What happens is that I stand at the beginning of worship, move to the center of the church in front of the first row of seats, and then—in a non-ritualistic manner—offer a welcome to all in the name of Jesus Christ our Lord. I also offer a special welcome to visitors and ask if they wouldn't mind introducing themselves.

Each week, surprisingly, they do. Introduce themselves, that is.

As one stands to speak, another will feel more confident about standing, and then still others will pop up, until we have several people, maybe 10 to 12 of them, waiting their turn. Often the ritual requires several minutes before the Call to Worship. What happens is that an usher hurries over with a microphone (and a welcome package) so that all can hear.

I sense that everyone enjoys this moment as much as I do. Even the youth, who on one side of the balcony are pretending not to notice.

What makes this time of worship so interesting?

First, of course, it's the places people come from. Australia, Greece, Singapore, the U.K., Korea, South Africa, and—last Sunday—Princeton, New Jersey. An audible murmur is heard when a far-off and exotic place is mentioned.

Princeton, New Jersey! Can you imagine?

The other reason this moment in worship is so interesting is that it reminds us each week of the global reach of the Christian church. If we had any doubts whatsoever that the church exists (and thrives) all around the world, this ritual—sorry, not sure what else to call it—reminds us that we do not exist alone, that every Sunday, on nearly every continent, people of faith are gathering and singing and listening and offering themselves in worship.

Last Sunday, much later in the service, as members and visitors alike came forward to receive the elements of communion, I was aware—as I am nearly every time we do this—that the family of God is far more varied than I sometimes imagine.

As I offered a small piece of bread, I said, "The body of Christ for you." And then I thought, "For God so loved the world—no, really, the whole world!"

Renewal is a gift

For nearly 15 years I have been involved in various ways with the Calvin Institute of Christian Worship, which, among many other things, makes grants to churches for worship. We used to call it "worship renewal," but now for various reasons say "vital worship." Either way, the grants amount to hundreds of thousands of dollars each year.

One of my responsibilities—I share this work with a wonderful group of colleagues who are seminary faculty and worship scholars from all over the U.S.—is to read grant proposals from churches. Reading dozens of grant proposals every year sounds at first like tedious work. And occasionally it can be. But most of the time, to my surprise and delight, it is exciting and energizing to read about all the ways churches in North America are trying to renew and revitalize their worship lives.

I sometimes find myself in tears at the creative ways that churches—and worship leaders—are using to meet the challenges they face. I come away from reading grant proposals thinking, "The church isn't dying. It has never been more alive." One year I could hardly wait to meet a particular grant recipient at the annual colloquium because I recognized in her extraordinary pastoral instincts. Pastors with her gifts do not come along every day.

Reading these proposals each year has had the unintended effect of helping me to keep in touch with the Christian church as it exists all over North America—with their struggles and challenges, as well as their creative ideas and solutions. Early on, it was clear that many churches were responding to the challenge of an aging membership by introducing a second service with a more contemporary expression of praise. The hope—in every case I can recall—was to engage the younger people.

Some churches are still doing that—still adding new services with contemporary worship styles— but the pace seems to have slowed considerably. Maybe all of the churches that have considered a change in worship style or adding another service with a different style have already done so. My sense is that it's difficult to find a church that has not at least attempted this strategy.

A year ago I noticed in the grant proposals, however, what may be a shift or a new trend altogether—namely, to bring two different services back together. The grant proposal that I recall most vividly wanted to take a year to bring two very different worshiping congregations back together in one space and at the same time.

After more than a decade of receiving worship grant proposals and distributing hundreds of thousands of U.S. dollars in grant money, Betty Grit at the Worship Institute published some of her findings or reflections on worship in the U.S. She calls these "proverbs"—or, in still other language, "the things we've learned."

- "Worship renewal cannot be produced or engineered by human ingenuity, but is a gift of God's Spirit. Renewal is a gift for which we pray, rather than an accomplishment we achieve."
- "Worship renewal mines the riches of Scripture and leads worshipers to deeper encounters with Christ and the gospel message."
- "Relationships (Christian fellowship, trust, forgiveness, and grace) are essential for worshiping together."
- "Worship involves all the senses."
- "Learning about worship is essential for renewal."
- "Worship renewal often takes place around the sacraments."
- "There is a hunger for worship renewal."

If you were to substitute the term "multicultural worship" for every time the term "worship renewal" is used, I think you have would have a dandy set of proverbs for the multicultural church:

- "Multicultural worship cannot be produced or engineered by human ingenuity, but is a gift of God's Spirit."
- "Multicultural worship mines the riches of Scripture and leads worshipers to deeper encounters with Christ and the gospel message."
- "Relationships are essential for worshiping together in a multicultural church."

- "Multicultural worship often takes place around the sacraments."
- "There is a hunger for multicultural worship."

What's astonishing to me about that list is precisely what has astonished me about the worship life of a thriving multicultural church in Switzerland—that the reasons for growth, life, vitality, and renewal have so little to do with a particular worship (and music) style.

I don't go to church much anymore

I like to tell family members and friends that I don't go to church much anymore. That usually gets their attention, and when they look puzzled, I like to say that I haven't attended regularly since 1980, when I stopped being a church member altogether. I have mostly good memories of going to church, I tell them, but for most of my adult life I have worked on Sundays.

This, of course, is where they begin to catch on. I was ordained in 1980, and now I work on Sunday. And I can't go to church like everyone else.

In any case, usually on vacation, I wake up on Sunday and think about going to church. But I have to admit that going to church has become a great deal more difficult than it used to be. For one thing, my parents are no longer making me go. For another thing, going to church now means getting up and getting out of the house on a day off.

Next, there is deciding what to wear. Really, what do people wear to church these days? I haven't gone to church in such a long time that I rarely think about the question. I haven't paid attention for ages. On a recent summer vacation in the U.S., I opted for shorts, but almost immediately regretted the decision. I felt uncomfortable, even though most of the other men, as it turned out, were also wearing shorts.

My mom and dad used to say that I should dress for church the way I would dress to go to the White House and meet the President. In adulthood, apparently, I have a hard time finding freedom from the law.

Singing as a member of a congregation is also much harder than I would have expected. I love to sing, but I should point out that loving to sing is different from singing well. I love to sing when no one, except maybe God and my granddaughter, can hear me. Where I sit most Sundays, no one can hear me, and I usually sing as loudly as I can, occasionally fumbling for my microphone to make sure it's on "mute."

On that summer Sunday recently when I got up and went to church, I was thrilled to find out that I knew the first hymn. It was "Be Thou My Vision." And so I started singing it enthusiastically, as though for God's and my granddaughter's enjoyment, only to discover that no one around me was singing. Not a single person. I looked and couldn't see any moving lips.

For a couple of stanzas I tried to create some musical excitement where I was standing, but finally I gave up when a couple of people turned around to find out what the croaking toad behind them looked like.

And then there was the message. I know a little about the degree of difficulty involved in preaching, so I was willing to give a lot of bonus points for sincerity and effort and conviction. But not even a lot of sincerity and effort and conviction can make listening bearable for 25 minutes.

I thought about leaving during the last hymn, but on that summer Sunday I noticed that a large group near me was already doing that. Maybe they were late for their brunch reservations. Instead, I decided— heroically—to stay all the way through the Benediction.

Here's the thing—and this may surprise you: I found that Sunday morning in worship to be far more helpful and eye-opening than I ever would have imagined. I now have a whole new level of respect for those who do it. I may even start going to church again.

I can be very critical about most things, but especially about the church. I seldom like the sermon. I can be picky about the music. Frankly, I can (and do) find fault with just about everything at church, even with the cookies at coffee hour. (When was the last time you had a really good cookie at a church coffee hour? Right, my point exactly.)

When people talk about spending eternity singing in the heavenly choir, I hate to admit it, but I don't look forward to it. I hope it's okay for me to admit that. My point is that I hope worship in heaven is a great deal better than it usually is down here.

So, what is it then that I find so memorable at the church I now serve? I don't know. I am still trying to put my finger on it.

Part of it, I think, is that no one tries very hard. What I mean is that worship isn't a show or a performance. No one gasps when a mistake is made. We aim for excellence, of course, and I feel bad about the mistakes we make. But everyone from pastors to worship leaders to members of the congregation are real, authentic, and genuine. And that goes a long way toward making the inevitable mistakes and miscues seem unimportant.

Another part of it, I think, is the blend of old and new. The people are sometimes given responses that date to the earliest days of the church, and then occasionally there are elements that might have been written yesterday. In this way, I feel connected to believers of all times and places, but I also sense that the faith is being newly expressed.

There is more, of course, like the relationships within the church that deepen over time, but I realize each Sunday, with some relief, that it doesn't take much. I'm really not that hard to please. I just want to know that I have been in the presence of God.

CHAPTER TEN

It's the Meal (Where Strangers Become Friends)

If music style does not predict a vital, thriving multicultural church (see the previous chapter), then maybe food can. I don't know the answer right now, but I am enjoying the research.

In spite of the jokes that are often made about church potlucks in the U.S.—with all of their green Jell-O salads, some even featuring tiny bits of suspended fruit—the food at these events is surprisingly good. That's my finding after years of research. And what's more, there's nothing like the promise of a meal to guarantee a larger than usual number of people at any church activity.

My experience is limited mainly to Presbyterian churches, of course, so maybe my data sample is too small to draw many conclusions. But my sense is that there is often very good food to be found at a church potluck—alongside the Jell-O salads and the tuna casseroles.

Just imagine, then, what a potluck at a multicultural church is like.

I suppose the quality may vary somewhat among these churches. The Netherlands, for example, is not noted for its distinctive cuisine, so no one comes to a potluck at my church keenly anticipating that the Dutch families will bring an authentic Dutch dish (whatever that would be). I suppose the same could be said for the English. No one keenly anticipates what our families from the U.K. might bring either. And this goes for a few other people groups around the world not known for their distinctive cuisines. On the other hand, there's nothing like having a few families from India who bring dishes that excite the palate and make the potluck interesting. Or families from China. Or Lebanon. Or Peru.

Frankly, the more varied the congregation, the more interesting the menu at the church potluck. My argument is not that we should aim for multicultural churches in order to have interesting potlucks, although that idea may have some merit. I think potlucks teach us another lesson.

I should not be surprised about how important church potlucks are—or the large crowds they typically draw—because it has always been around a table that the body of Christ has become visible. It is in the breaking of bread, we typically say, that we recognize the risen Christ present among us. Sometimes we even say that at table we are able to catch a glimpse of the *heavenly* banquet—or as a favorite old hymn puts it, a "foretaste of glory divine."

The various Christian traditions mean something different of course about exactly what happens at the table (and what the spoken words really mean). A lot of battles have been fought and a lot schisms have occurred over all of that, but all traditions speak about the importance of a table, a simple meal, and a few carefully chosen words. In the moment, frankly, I never try to think carefully about what is happening. As I stand behind the table, I never do a mental review of what has been said and written over the years about the sacrament. It is usually enough for me to be fully present, to be caught up in the mystery, to remember that I am, as the apostle Paul once put it, a steward "of God's mysteries" (1 Cor. 4:1).

The church has always looked forward to coming together around a table—in worship, of course, but also in the church social hall, and in the homes of members—and what we believe is that *something* happens there, that sharing a meal can be and often is a deeply spiritual activity, that we can be changed. In spite of the vastly different language Christians use to describe what happens in a shared meal, we seem to be aware that in the meal is a mystery, something to approach with care and wonder and awe.

I heard someone joke one time that if men were expected to prepare the meal (and do the clean-up afterwards), then the theological thinking about all of this might have developed in an entirely different direction. But gender roles aside—and every culture seems to have them—there is something about coming together to share a meal, something that transcends the act of receiving nourishment, something that seems full of spiritual meaning and significance.

It's that spiritual meaning and significance that I have come to recognize as crucially important for the multicultural church. If people from a variety of racial and ethnic and cultural backgrounds are ever going to come together in a meaningful way, my fear is that it's not going to be around a doctrinal statement, no matter how well-crafted it is, but around a table. It's at the table that we find our oneness in Christ.

When God came among us, it was not in the form of a confession or creed, but a person. Why do I have such a difficult time remembering that? It's on those days when I look for theological unity that I experience my greatest despair about the church. But it seems clear to me now that I have been looking in the wrong place.

The place to look has been in front of me all the time.

The biblical roots of hospitality

All four Gospels contain stories about Jesus sharing a meal. Some of those meals, maybe the most important ones, are with his disciples, but occasionally meals take place with others as well.

Jesus' mealtime habits must have been a topic of conversation—and certainly much gossip too— because there are references to meals with unsavory characters, people with whom an aspiring religious leader who cares about his reputation might not want to be seen. His meals at the homes of tax collectors seemed to draw the most attention, but criticism occurred in other situations as well.

In Luke 7 Jesus was having a meal at the home of a Pharisee when a woman, described only as "a sinner," washed Jesus' feet with her tears, wiped those same feet with her hair, and then anointed those feet with perfume. The disapproval from those who witnessed all of this, not surprisingly, was swift, but Jesus seemed moved by what happened and sent the woman away with the words "your faith has saved you; go in peace" (Luke 7:50).

A great deal happens around the table, not always having to do with the food.

The story of Jesus in the home of Mary and Martha (Luke 10)—where Martha grows irritated over her sister's refusal to help—is probably remembered as much for the window into first-century domestic life as it is for the teaching it provides. Jesus wisely stayed out of the dispute between the two sisters, until Martha demanded that he rebuke Mary.

So, reluctantly, as I imagine it, Jesus says, "Martha, Martha, you are worried and distracted by many things; there is need of only one thing. Mary has chosen the better part, which will not be taken away from her" (Luke 10:41–42).

Coming together for a meal, Jesus seems to say, is not first of all about the food.

Meals in the Middle East today, as they were in ancient Near Eastern history, are important for several reasons. They were occasions when families gathered—not mom, dad, and the kids, maybe, but extended families, larger gatherings—and they could also be occasions when hospitality to strangers was demonstrated. Meals and hospitality seem to be closely, perhaps inextricably, linked in the biblical narrative.

In the Book of Genesis there are several references to hospitality, but none more striking than the story in chapter 18, where Abraham and Sarah welcome three strangers and then go to considerable lengths to demonstrate openness and welcome to them.

In that culture, it is important to remember, there was no service industry to offer meals and lodging to weary travelers—no Quality Inns and Suites offering a "complimentary breakfast" with your stay—and yet there is something in the story that suggests the normative nature of what Abraham and Sarah did, that this was how things were supposed to be, not only in that culture but beyond.

I sometimes wonder why this story does not figure more prominently in the Western, Christian imagination. Christians tend to find biblical stories or even relatively obscure verses and treat them as though they contain important and timeless truths, but we seem to overlook or neglect the power and mystery of what took place in this particular story, as though it has no claim on us and nothing to teach us. I read somewhere that there are no fewer than 36 places in the Old Testament where we are commanded to show hospitality to strangers. And yet, in all my years of church-going and Sunday school classes, I don't remember much, if any, emphasis on this particular truth.

Even the Epistle to the Hebrews, in the New Testament, apparently refers to the story of Abraham and Sarah's hospitality when it says, "Do not neglect to show hospitality to strangers, for by doing that some have entertained angels without knowing it" (13:2). In the act of hospitality there is a divine-human connection. The meal becomes more than a meal. God is present.

When Jesus gives the litany of behaviors that he expects to find in his followers—"when I was hungry and you gave me food, I was thirsty and you gave me something to drink"—this matter of welcoming the stranger, hospitality, is right there in the middle of it: "I was a stranger and you welcomed me" (Matt. 25:35).

We seem to understand the other expectations Jesus mentions fairly well—the ones about the hungry, thirsty, naked, sick, and so on—but this other one always seems to be much more difficult, as though it's a stretch for us. Why is that?

I was a stranger and you welcomed me.

This expectation wasn't hard to understand in Jesus' first-century world, or in the world of Abraham and Sarah several centuries prior, but it is in many Christian communities today. And in many churches as well.

When we welcome the stranger, when we offer hospitality to our guests, it is as though we are welcoming Christ himself.

One August evening

During a very hot and humid August several years ago, on a mission trip to northern Israel, my nephew and I went for a walk in an Arab village. The group I was leading had worked hard all day at a Christian school in the village, and after dinner my nephew and I decided to get out and see a little of where we were living. Even though this trip was pre-9/11, we were somewhat apprehensive. Everyone had told us before we left the U.S. to be careful.

Our host, an Arab Christian pastor and the founder of the school where we were working, told us that we should not be afraid to walk the streets of his village or to enter any home in the village. He was quite emphatic about this and stated over and over again that we would be safe, but that hardly eased our fears. We were well aware that we were in a foreign culture—what with the Muslim call to prayer waking us early every morning—and so we were guarded in our behavior.

As it turned out, we were not alone in our walk. The setting of the hot summer sun seemed to bring everyone out of their stuffy homes for cooler air, and one resident of the village spotted us, came over, and sensing our thirst or planning to kill us—we didn't know which—invited us in for a glass of water. He seemed to know little English, and we knew next to no Arabic, but we understood the offer of hospitality.

I wish I could say that I had no fears about this, but I was feeling particularly responsible during the trip for my nineteen-year-old nephew and was determined to bring him home unharmed to his mother, even if my life was required in the process. So, I hesitated and nearly said no to the invitation, but the villager prevailed on us, and eventually we relented, as though we were doing him a favor by entering his home and drinking his water.

It was not the last time on that August visit that we experienced what can only be called extraordinary hospitality. A family in that village even invited our entire mission team to their daughter's wedding reception on a Saturday evening. Everywhere we went we were warmly welcomed by Christians and Muslims alike. Everything I had been told about the importance of welcoming the stranger in that part of the world seemed to be true.

And frankly, I was impressed, mostly because I could not have imagined anything similar happening in my own community back in the U.S. Invite a couple of thirsty-looking Arabs, possibly Muslims, people I had never met before, people I had been taught not to trust, into my home for a drink of water (or to my daughter's wedding reception)?

Not in any neighborhood where I have ever lived. I probably would have thought about calling the police instead.

From hostility to hospitality

No one has been more helpful to me in my understanding of Christian hospitality over the years than the late Henri Nouwen, who has written so thoughtfully and well about the spiritual life. In his wonderful book *Reaching Out: Three Movements of the Spiritual Life*, Nouwen argues that one of the movements of the spiritual life is "from hostility to hospitality."

When Christians, at least in the West, encounter a stranger, our default response, according to Nouwen, is to be afraid, to move into a defensive posture. The assumption is that the stranger will try to pull one over on us, to take something that belongs to us, or to harm us. We can be pushing a cart down the aisle at the grocery store or strolling through an Arab village after sunset, and our instinct will be the same.

Someone is bound to be lurking in the shadows, and that person means to do us harm.

What Nouwen suggests—and I have been pondering these words ever since I first read them more than 30 years ago—is that our faith calls us to something different. To welcome the stranger means moving past our fear and creating space—what Nouwen calls "free, friendly space," what we might call life-giving space. I suppose there will inevitably be occasions and situations when fear is warranted, when we should be afraid, when it would be foolish not to protect ourselves, but Nouwen has something more in mind.

His argument, as I understand it, is that a Christian, a follower of Christ, must learn to see strangers as Abraham and Sarah saw them—in other words, as angels, as messengers from God, as people we might want to know, as people from whom we could learn, if only we could set aside our fear and hostility.

I don't think I saw this clearly at the beginning of my work in Zürich, but I see it now: the only way to thrive in my role as pastor of an international church, the only way to thrive as a member of a church like this, is to recognize that other people, other cultures, have something to teach me, that my own faith will be deepened in our relationship. What's required isn't suspicion, but openness, a willingness to see others as God sees them.

Newcomers to Switzerland, I've noticed, go through a predictable pattern of adjustment which usually begins with fear and isolation. The initial paperwork, for example, can be daunting. The Swiss love orderliness, not least when it comes to immigration, but the sheer volume of it all and the level of detail can be overwhelming.

And the result is that there is a tendency, at least at the beginning, to seek out the safety of others who look and sound like we do, which is why some expats move into a kind of bubble with fellow expats and never venture very far from it.

There is also a tendency in the first days and weeks after the move to miss everything that was left behind—to search grocery store shelves, for example, for food items that for some reason are not available in this new country. No cheddar cheese? Really? In a land of cheese?

The initial fear and isolation will often, though not always, give way to something else—namely, an idealization of the new country.

At this new stage everything the Swiss do seems so well thought out and organized and, well, perfect! Even the air is cleaner and the lakes are purer! The trains run on time! And of course there is a postcard view in every direction!

Newcomers find themselves wondering why the country they left behind hasn't adopted some of the obviously superior patterns and behaviors. Wouldn't it be so much better for the environment, for example, if everyone reused their grocery bags? How hard would it be to come to the store with the same bags that were used the last time—and the time before that?

It has occurred to me that the immigrant experience is a little like falling in love. After an initial hesitation or awkwardness, everything about the other seems so wonderful and enchanting and delightful!

And the feeling, I must say, is very nice, while it lasts.

Inevitably, though, that initial infatuation dims a bit and gives way to something more sustainable. Let's call it a grateful acceptance. There is a great deal to admire about Switzerland, and there is a great deal the U.S. could learn from Swiss habits and customs (beyond reusable shopping bags). But Switzerland is a tiny country with a relatively tiny population.

And so, slowly, there is a realization that the two cultures are not really comparable. Switzerland needs to be loved and appreciated for what it is.

As the pastor of an international, multicultural church, I have found myself going through all or most of these feelings. I admit to some fear when I started. The strong initial reservations about me and my biography (and my yoga) created some hesitation and feelings of isolation. My first sermons were cautious and tentative. My worship leadership was unnaturally reserved.

Not only that, but at the beginning I longed for an evening at home, to get away, to breathe. I even looked forward to watching the BBC and hearing the comforting sounds of the English language.

Slowly, though, I found myself telling people back in the U.S. that I had fallen in love with this culture and this church. "What's not to love?" I would say, blushing, or whatever a man my age does when he's in love.

The people were warm and welcoming, they were inviting me over to their homes so often that all of my free evenings were filling up, and best of all they seemed genuinely interesting. They were people I wanted to know, people I wanted to spend time with. Everything about life in this new church seemed novel and special! I couldn't get enough.

Even their bad habits—every person who has ever fallen in love can identify with this—seemed absolutely charming at the beginning.

And then, finally—I don't remember when it happened—my feelings seem to have given way to something more sustainable. "Falling in love" has given way to simply loving these people, knowing that they are people I want to be with, recognizing that they are teaching me as much as or more than I am teaching them, seeing evidence of God's work in the world in the work we are doing together.

Swiss hospitality

John Koenig, in his remarkable and scholarly work *New Testament Hospitality: Partnership with Strangers as Promise and Mission*, reflects at length on the Greek word *philoxenia*, which is the word used in the New Testament for hospitality and which literally means "love of strangers."

Koenig tells us that the word refers not only to what *we* might offer to strangers, but to what *they* might offer to us. As Koenig describes the host and stranger relationship, there is a kind of delight the host feels in the act of hospitality.

During our brief time in Zürich, my wife and I have been invited into the homes of more church members than ever before, in the more than 36 years of my ministry. Of course, that's due partly to the prohibitive cost of dining out in a city like Zürich. For most people, restaurants are for special occasions; other gatherings happen in the home.

And partly all of those invitations are due to the nature of a vital, thriving church in a decidedly secular context. To spend time with people who are believers, who speak the same faith language, I have learned, is something of a luxury. People here look for and cherish occasions when faith is not considered a taboo topic. They are genuinely excited to make the discovery that someone they know—a neighbor, a co-worker!—is a believer.

Typically, in these social situations, we have tried to bring a gift—a bottle of wine, chocolate (this is Switzerland, after all), or even flowers. But the gift in these situations is not what we bring or even the meal that is offered to us, even though the meals have been, without exception, lovingly prepared and thoughtfully served. No, the gift is what happens at table—in the process of getting to know each other, in the exchange of ideas, in listening to stories.

Because I am a pastor, I have come to expect conversations of a certain kind. Having the pastor over for dinner ordinarily means at least a little (and frequently a great deal of) "church talk," which is how my wife gamely refers to it.

To be fair, it's a safe subject. The church, after all, is how we happen to know each other. And so conversation often begins with this shared experience.

But often, after we get the "church talk" out of the way, we will hear stories of such depth and grace—about the death of a loved one, for example, or the serious illness of a child or a parent, or the unexpected difficulty of moving to this new culture—that would not have been shared, surely not at such an early point in the relationship and not in such depth, if I were not a pastor.

I count it a privilege that over the years I have heard many such stories. Early in my ministry, when my pastoral identity was still forming, when I was still startled and a little embarrassed to be addressed as "pastor," I confess that I often did not know what to do with these stories. I was uncomfortable when people would share a confidence with me, something they had most likely not told another human being. Now, years later, I try to receive these stories, these intimacies, as the gifts they are, as a form of communion.

The thing is, in a multicultural and international church, these stories are often surprising and astonishing. They involve subjects that are far from my experience. They introduce me to cultures that I know little about.

Asking a couple from India where and how they met seemed innocent enough. As with the "Where are you from?" question, I assumed that by asking I was simply being friendly and interested. In a U.S. setting, we would have expected to hear a story about a college romance or a workplace flirtation or an online dating site. Instead, on this occasion, we were surprised to hear the tender and complicated story of an arranged marriage. We hear about arranged marriages all the time now, but this first one came as something of a surprise.

The couple told us that the custom, so important to their parents, would probably come to an end with them, with their generation. Their children were being raised in another culture, after all, with an entirely different set of expectations. They seemed to be aware of how strange the story of an arranged marriage might sound to someone like me who is thoroughly Westernized, but they assured us that it was in many ways a wonderful experience, one that they did not regret, one that might be superior in some ways to the Western notion of "falling in love" as a prerequisite for marriage.

Still, we were aware that we were hearing an unusual and deeply personal story, and we received it as a gift, which is how it was intended. The meal was excellent and different, as always, from anything we had experienced before, but so was the conversation and the intimacy and the recognition that our relationship now included this additional bond of shared stories. We knew each other afterward in a way that we did not know each other before that meal. Something happened that evening that drew us together, that mattered more than the food that was served.

The more difficult thing

I have mentioned that the act of serving communion in a multiracial, multiethnic church can be breath-taking. In fact, I find that it never grows old. But after the first few times I began to sense something else—namely, that seeing the miracle of a communion service at a church like mine is almost too easy.

Just about every first-time visitor notices it too.

I do not deny the miracle. It was and continues to be a highlight of my ministry, and I have had many highlights along the way, but seeing it, noticing it, paying attention to it is almost too easy. It's like seeing a beautiful sunset and then feeling gratitude for God's good creation. I think just about anybody can do that. I mean, if you're open to experiences like that, if you have even the tiniest bit of spiritual awareness, then seeing God in sunsets is easy or at least possible. Sunsets (and sunrises too) are an entry-level stage in the spiritual life. If you've gotten that far, good for you.

What I find myself doing, however, is wanting more—with sunsets and communion services and a hundred other, more mundane experiences of life. Maybe I should just receive the gift of the communion service and be happy about it. Maybe I should go home on a Sunday afternoon, feel grateful for the experience, take a nap, and be done with it. I suppose there's no prize for making the spiritual life harder and more difficult than it is.

But I find that I can't do that. Maybe it's my theological training, maybe it's my inability to accept the most obvious explanation for anything. Whatever it is, I have tried to challenge myself to see beneath the surface of things, even the good things, even the things that don't always lend themselves to analysis, like coming together around a table.

What in the world is going on? Why do I find myself in tears nearly every time I offer the bread to members of my church? Why do I find myself so lost in the moment that I fail to notice how long communion serving actually takes? Some people, I should note, have complained about it, have felt the need to call or write, have suggested ways we could "speed things up," but I can honestly say that I have never experienced serving communion as "taking too long." I usually find myself a little sad, in fact, when the last person has received that tiny bit of bread from me, when I turn back to the table and survey the mess we have made, when I finally look out at the congregation and say, "Let us pray."

On communion Sunday at my church something remarkable happens. As the Bible puts it, "People will come from east and west, from north and south and will eat in the kingdom of God" (Luke 13:29). For one brief moment (a lot longer, according to a few people) we look like the gathering on that first Pentecost or that gathering described in Revelation 7 where every nation, tribe, and tongue stands before the Lamb. We have experienced the hospitality of God, the hospitality that in turn frees us to invite and welcome others. We become involved in Jesus' own work of drawing people together.

Rowan Williams, the former Archbishop of Canterbury, in his book *Being Christian: Baptism, Bible, Eucharist, Prayer,* has written about "that wonderful alternation in the Gospels between Jesus giving hospitality and receiving hospitality [which] shows us something absolutely essential about the Eucharist. We are the guests of Jesus. We are there because he asks us, and because he wants our company. At the same time we are set free to invite Jesus into our lives and literally to receive him into our bodies in the Eucharist. His welcome gives us the courage to open up to him. . . . We are welcomed and we welcome; we welcome God and we welcome our unexpected neighbours."

"Our unexpected neighbors"—those are the people with whom I have been doing ministry for nearly four decades.

This is heady stuff for someone like me. For more years than I care to remember I have been hoping for some confirmation that my work matters. I have wanted to know that all of my evening meetings and lost holidays and abbreviated weekends have counted for something. I have wanted to know that time spent away from my family, attending to crises within other families, has really been worth it. I have wanted to know that my ministry has made even the tiniest bit of difference.

All of this may sound like whining, and quite possibly it is, because I do a fair amount of it, but every pastor who has been at this work as long as I have, or even for a few months, will recognize the truth in what I am saying: Being a pastor is not like being a house painter. There isn't much to admire at the end of the day. Even on the best days, I wonder if there is anything I can point to, solid evidence that the kingdom is any closer to being a reality.

But then, on communion Sundays, I see it. Or I think I see it.

I catch a glimpse of the kingdom of God, and I don't know exactly how to put this, but that glimpse of something that I can't quite put into words, that may or may not be real, that seems just beyond my reach, keeps me going. That glimpse, I must say, has made all these years of ministry seem worthwhile. That glimpse may be the best thing I have ever been permitted to see. If I die today, I can say that I was given a glimpse before I died of what was to come.

At the beginning, around the time of my ordination, I felt such wonder at being called to the ministry of word and sacrament. But it's hard work, harder than I ever imagined it would be, with inevitable moments and sometimes whole seasons of despair, and the temptation over the years has been strong to let it go and find real work, with regular hours and pay and benefits, with results that are visible to the naked eye.

And now, truthfully, I can say that I have seen something that I've been waiting all my life to see.

Afterword

Doug Brouwer and I grew up at a time when rock-and-roll bands toured with warm-up acts. We have been friends and colleagues for almost as long. And I've been given the privilege to talk about his book.

How to Become a Multicultural Church is a fresh, candid, insightful—even entertaining—glimpse into what it's like to labor outside the bounds of one's comfort zone. More specifically, what it's like to do ministry within the context of an international congregation in a foreign city.

I may be only a warm-up act—or a show-closer—but you should know that, like the author, I am a road warrior myself when it comes to international ministry and the multicultural scene. In fact, I walked in Doug's shoes for over nine years in Zürich prior to his arrival. So I know the territory that Doug guides you through, and I can assure you that his guidance is sound and credible.

What has made reading Doug's book so enjoyable for me is revisiting people and places I've known and loved (mostly) for nearly two decades. How much fun it is to see them through the eyes of a colleague who is a relative newcomer to this scene! As most veterans (of anything) know, once those things that at first were new and exotic have become familiar and commonplace, it's easy to become jaded. That's why I'm grateful to Doug for providing us with a journal of his first eighteen months overseas. He has reminded me of so many lessons I learned the hard way years ago as I was trying to stay afloat in unfamiliar waters. Don't I wish this book had been available when I was in way over my head!

From my own ministry experience—in Belfast, Northern Ireland; in Zürich and Lugano, Switzerland; and in a small church on a university campus in Minnesota—I can say that every word Doug has written rings true. Rarely have I smiled and nodded as much as I did when reading this narrative. Yes, it is actually possible to *enjoy* a book about church work. Not only are these characters and encounters believable, but they resemble many of those that I have had. And I've felt the same sensations and drawn similar conclusions during my own roller-coaster ride in international ministry.

My wife, Susan, came up with a good description of the three stages one passes through when moving from one country/culture to another. It provides a useful template for understanding what the Brouwers have gone through since leaving the United States and settling in Switzerland:

1. *The Awesome Stage:* "Look at that! Isn't it wonderful?" This describes the sense of awe and wonder that the newcomer experiences for the first few weeks or months of foreign residency.
2. *The Annoying Stage:* "Why can't they do it the right way?" In other words, why can't they do it *my* way? Once the foreign honeymoon is over, the irritating reality of having to adjust to new ways of doing things hits home.
3. *The Acceptance Stage:* "This is the way things are done here . . . and I rather like it." After months of learning the local ropes, you form new patterns and habits and create a new comfort zone.

As I took the delightful journey through Doug's book, it struck me how relevant this saga is for all people, not just church folk, at this time in history, when we are being challenged to adapt to living in a global community and are caught up in crises of our own. Today's political, religious, and secular leaders are having to deal with the unprecedented problems caused by the mass migrations of asylum-seekers, refugees, and other displaced groups of people. These leaders are pressed to find ways to accommodate newcomers with different values and behaviors. Even though similar crises have arisen throughout history, the current challenges are expanding exponentially. With this latest wave of change, no country or community will remain untouched. No longer is it a luxury of choice to engage and assimilate with those who are quite different from us.

As I write this, those in positions of authority are stymied about what they can do to manage this mounting storm of pluralism and ideological confrontation. There are wars and rumors of war, rising ethnic and racial tensions, commercial and financial volatility, and, perhaps most dramatic of all, the clashing values among three of the world's greatest religions. This leaves us wondering what can be done to prevent our supposedly "civilized" societies from bursting apart at the seams. If ever there was a need for new solutions to stabilize potentially volatile relationships, it is now.

All of this makes Doug's narrative timely and relevant, reminding us that we can only do what we are capable of doing, whether it's at the congregational level or in other arenas. In the midst of such uncertainty, anxiety can take over and rob us of personal joy and fulfillment. That's why it's best to know our limitations and do our utmost within them. Rather than allowing ourselves to be overwhelmed by the complexities surrounding us, and either withdrawing or overreacting, we must find handles of hope to help us regain stability and discover how wonderful it can be when good and decent people, regardless of background or cultural biases, band together on common ground to reach beyond the confining borders of familiarity and homogeneity.

Within these pages, Doug has provided us with an itinerary for finding a place where regret over losing what "has been" is replaced by excitement about what "will be." If we don't learn the lessons that he has learned and continues to learn, our assumptions may leave us stranded in survival camps, content to hang out with our own kind but unmotivated to implement changes for the better. This is not the vision of the future that we hear Jesus describing in the New Testament. He envisions a day when we will lay aside our differences and unite in our common humanity and faith in God.

Doug and I have learned the same lesson during our time at the International Protestant Church of Zürich. There are two essentials for those of us who follow Christ: the lordship of Jesus and the authority of the Bible. No matter where we've come from or where we presently find ourselves, these are the two legs on which the church stands. Everything else is negotiable. It has to be.

Thank you, Doug, for taking the risk at this stage in your life and ministry to lift our eyes to see the bigger picture, where the small ripples of change will soon be massive waves breaking on every shore.

RICHARD A. DAVIS

Acknowledgments

I wrote this book to better understand ministry in a multicultural setting, and I wasn't bashful about asking for help. Some people read chapters in early stages, and others simply listened to me as I tried to make sense of what felt like an enormous challenge. I am grateful to everyone who was a part of this project.

Among those who read chapters at an early stage is Richard A. Davis, who served as pastor of the International Protestant Church of Zürich for nine years and was elected pastor emeritus when he left. He established many of the norms and expectations that allow this multicultural church to thrive.

William Dyrness, professor of theology and culture at Fuller Theological Seminary, colleague, and friend, provided guidance and ideas at a critical point in the project. Like any good teacher, he was not only supportive, but also pointed to new paths that a wise student might want to explore.

My writers group—Patty Jehle, Kathryn Stok, and Ming Goh, all members of IPC—combined encouragement and honesty in their feedback at an early stage. I hope I've done a little of the same for them in their own writing.

Acknowledgments

I am grateful to dear friends Mary R. Talen and Thomas B. Dozeman, whom I have known for more than 40 years. On this topic, as with so many others over the years, they helped me to clarify my thinking and to say what I mean. Family members Marvin Hage and J. M. van der Laan were also generous with comments and insights, and like relatives everywhere, they did not hesitate to mention what sounded lame and unconvincing.

With this book, Eerdmans Publishing Company has now published my fourth book about ministry, and I am proud of our long association. Mary Hietbrink, someone whose editorial smarts I have admired since college newspaper days, was my conscience, guide, and friend, as she was for the previous three books. We have done good work together.

And finally, the three women in my life who know me best and love me anyway—my wife and two daughters—were also helpful in the project, and I am more grateful to them than I can possibly express. I should mention that they have done far more than read chapters and offer observations; they have walked with me in my ministry for much of their lives, absorbing all its experiences, both the good and the bad, right along with me.